HEROIN RISING
A TALE OF TRUE TERROR

WRITTEN BY T.A. BECHEL
EDITED BY EOIN FINNEGAN

T.A. Bechel Fiction
Wood River, Il 62095

For More info, visit: TABechel.com

ISBN-13: 978-1530066421

ISBN-10: 1530066425

Heroin Rising: A Tale of True Terror Copyright © 2015
by T.A. Bechel
Cover art Copyright © 2015 by Mark Mauer

Dedication

I dedicate this to those that stood by my side and those I severely wronged. You guys loved me the best, but I managed to treat you the worst. Grandma Bechel, wherever you are in this never-ending universe full of star dust, thank you for the lessons of life. Christina, not sure where I'd be without you, but today I'm glad it's with you. Mom without you, I wouldn't be a part of this mad, mad world - thank you. Beckie and Mark, we have not always seen eye to eye but thank you for all you have done for the kids and me. Kevin, the strange thing is we have always helped one another, and you offered an ear and sometimes a voice when I didn't want to hear it but needed it. Phil and Kyle all I can say is thank you. Tim, Gordon, and Aaron you guys are simply amazing. Gary, John, Connie, and Mike, your presence will be forever etched in my life. Justin, you always stuck by my side – knowing you were a reliable friend helped tremendously. Pat our late night pillow talk sessions offered laughter when it was greatly needed. A.J., you were a friend when I needed guidance the most, I just was not able to see it at the time. As for all of you that turned your back when the darkness overran my life, I forgive you. (This is a joke. Stick around madness long enough you too will find yourself just as <u>mad</u>, if not worse).

WARNING

For those in active addiction or early recovery from drug and alcohol addiction, there are graphic details recounting drug/alcohol use in descriptive detail. These may serve as triggers for some.

Introduction

What do you want to do with your life? When I was asked that in fifth grade, my response was, "To make a difference in the world." When I was asked that question again when I was in my first rehab, I was not sure how to answer it. Looking back, I can honestly say sometimes I have to ask what my desires were or in a more correct sense, my priorities. Gandhi once said, "Action expresses priorities." I think there is a lot of truth to that quote today, but at one point in my life, I would have told you to go piss off if I heard it. It seems like everywhere I turn there is something crazy taking place. We have a political system that appears to be falling completely apart. Someone told me the other day that since America's legal inception in 1776, we have had only twenty-one years with no conflict of war. If this is true, it makes me want to be even better as each day comes and goes.

One of the reasons I was not able to answer the question of what I wanted to do with my life was because of information like twenty-one years with no conflict scaring the living hell out of me – fear. Think about it for a minute. We live on one planet with an estimated seven billion people, and a majority of us are fighting something or someone. Someone like me that struggled with drug and alcohol addiction usually fights himself on a day to day basis along with most of the people we come into contact with. The pressures of fitting in, being successful, making our parents proud, or whatever the case may be, played a massive role in my priorities when I started taking legally prescribed opiates. I smoked weed and probably drank too much, but once I started taking those stupid pills, the dark clouds started rolling in. I was probably an asshole from time to time, but once I started taking those legally prescribed opiates everything started spiraling out of control so quickly my family and I were not prepared physically, mentally, or emotionally to handle the shit-storm about to rain down on all of us.

I have written this book for those who are addicted, their family, and friends, as a way to convey a real story so somebody, even if just one, can relate and find something useful. This has been suggested by a dear friend, who read this before it was published, as a survival guide for those deeply rooted in drug and alcohol addiction, especially those completely woven in the cross hairs of opiate addiction like heroin. I am not sure if it is a survival guide, but I do give insight to the almost unforgivable mistakes that I had made along with the recently personal triumphs I have achieved. The only way I can take advantage of these words is to be completely honest. My words will sometimes be kind or brutally unkind, but I assure you they are only explaining the unnecessary relationship I had with drugs and alcohol especially the relationship I developed with heroin that almost destroyed my family and left me for dead. Unlike many others, I have made it out alive from a grip so tight that I thought suicide was the only escape, a way to save my family from the desolation that consumed me every day.

Something bigger than me helped me find a way to love and care for myself that I thought I had lost. Whether that something was or is a God, a mighty Circuit Judge, a mercilessly honest Probation Officer, a few friends and family that had to force themselves to stay with me through the worst, or the idea of leaving my children behind with no father, and leaving an excellent mother to care for them by herself is up for debate depending on who you ask. Equally, they all have played their part in my life and the successes I embrace every morning that I get to wake up. Throughout this recount of my life, I have either changed names of individuals or left them out.

I contemplated writing and sharing this with anyone kind enough to read it. Then I thought to myself, if anyone anywhere on Earth could use this for some form of solace in their life, a beacon of light, to prevent them from experiencing what I did, or a way to build strength and develop a future for themselves or their loved ones, then why wouldn't I share it? One of my goals in life is to continue writing fiction, mostly like horror. My story is like many others that have shared pain similar to mine. I wish all of you that struggle, the addicts and their families and friends, a better, happier, and healthier life. Please know, I am not famous, but I was once infamous.

Chapter 1
Birth of an Addict

"I gotta find her weed!" I thought to myself as I scoured my mom's mother's bedroom. That's right, my grandma.

By the time my friends and I were fifteen years old, they had already smoked weed and I had not. I was at my mom's for the weekend, so I didn't want to be the only one that hadn't smoked, so I took the opportunity to do just that. My friends would tell me how great the feeling was, and my interest was certainly piqued. At fifteen, things changed so much from junior high. I was a straight-A student who played basketball, baseball, and participated in the Science Club and National Junior Honor Society but it all started slipping away when I moved to another school, AGAIN, and began to lose interest in my academics.

I grew up with my family that some may classify as dysfunctional on both sides. My parents decided to call it quits when I was four years old, so there was always a struggle between the two I always seemed to get tossed into. I love my parents and all of my family, but before I went to my mom's this particular weekend, my dad and I fought before I left, as usual. I was going to a school I really didn't want to go to, and I felt I didn't have any real friends there. Finding my grandma's weed wasn't just me being nosy; it became a mission for me to forget about my worries, if even for just a little while.

I found it. It was tucked away nicely behind an unopened tissue box in a small, half-dollar sized red Tupperware bowl with a clear lid. I dug an old pack of cigarettes out of the trash and took the cellophane. I took three pinches from the mini Tupperware bowl and carefully placed it back behind the tissue box. I rolled up the pot-filled cellophane and put it in my fifth pocket. Then I quickly went and asked my grandfather for a ride to my mom's house because I wanted to get this over with.

The funny thing is that my grandma and grandpa were not married any longer, and his girlfriend lived there at the time. It was always funny explaining it to my friends, their situation.

Grandpa drove me to my mom's with no suspicions that I had just pinched some pot from his ex-wife's stash.

My mom was working late and told me earlier that she would be going out after she got off. My younger brother was with his dad for the weekend, and I was all alone. I was afraid to smoke weed for the first time in front of my friends because I had seen some of them cough until they puked as everyone laughed at them. My brilliant plan was falling into place as I was about to get stoned for the very first time. I didn't have any paraphernalia, so I made a foiley; I only knew how to do this because I watched some of my friends make one before.

I placed the weed on the table, next to the aluminum pipe, and I took a deep breath. I took the white Bic out of my pocket I had also taken from my grandma's room, setting it on the table. As I sat at the table, I remember looking around the kitchen. The walls were stained with grease, the sink was full of dirty dishes, and the drywall was swollen from getting so hot in the house. My mom didn't have central air; summers were absolutely brutal in that house.

I tried talking myself out of smoking, but I thought of my dad and how he and his girlfriend made me move from one school district to another and how they always yelled at me; I loved to blame. I said screw it. I packed the homemade bowl with the sticky green that my grandma unknowingly donated to my cause as I placed it to my lips.

I flicked the Bic three times before I was able to

put the flame to the end of the bowl. I took a huge puff. Before I could inhale all the smoke, I began coughing like my friends did. My eyes went cross-eyed, and my head felt heavy all of a sudden. *Cough....cough...cough.* I put my forehead on the table and prayed that I would quit coughing.

My eyes were watering as I lifted my head up from the table. My vision was blurry as I wiped the liquid I refused to call tears from my cheeks and looked around the room. "Woahhhh," I said.

I continued to smoke beyond my limits. When I finished, I took the cellophane and foiley placing them in a bigger piece of aluminum foil, formed it into a ball, and buried the evidence deep in the trash.

For the first time in my life, I no longer had to worry about how awkward I felt at my dad's house or how misunderstood I thought I was. I didn't reflect on whether girls would like me; I thought about nothing. I finally found a way to live in the moment. I made my way to my bedroom then laid on the bed watching a basketball game on TV - on mute for some reason. I kept feeling like I was floating off of the bed and finding myself in the basketball game. Every noise I would hear would break my trance, and I kept thinking it was my mom. I'd sit straight up and yell for her but no answer. I never thought the feeling was going to end. I kept thinking to myself that I was going to get caught.

At some point, before my mom got home, whatever time that was, I fell asleep. When I woke up the next morning, my first thought was, "I'm gonna do that again."

If I had known that I was developing a pattern to avoid life and the way I felt about myself, I would have stopped smoking right then and there. I didn't stop, as the trouble was only about to begin.

My dad and I were constantly fighting. I questioned everything he said along with his girlfriend.

Some really bizarre things were happening, and I never felt quite right in that house with my dad, his girlfriend, her daughter, and my half-sister. I am not sure if it was an inner rebel that was causing the problems or if it was that my dad and his girlfriend were controlling. For reputation's sake, I like to think it was an inner rebel. We all want to be a badass, right?

I went to my mom's for Christmas break for about a week and a half in my sophomore year. When I got back to my dad's around 8:30 p.m. on a Sunday, I walked through the kitchen door to see a counter full of dishes. I took my book bag to my bedroom thinking to myself that I was glad that I didn't have to do all those dishes. Then I came up from my room and started playing a game on the computer. It got so awkward in our house that none of us actually talked. We tried to avoid each other at all costs. On this eventful Sunday evening, all of the pent-up frustrations were about to be unleashed by my dad and me.

I sat and played the computer game, I tried shooting the alien invasion with my starship when my dad walked in. He stood directly next to me with a cigarette in his right hand.

"You're going to do those dishes before you go to bed tonight," he said.

Instantly I was on the defensive. He TOLD me that I was going to do the dishes. I just turned sixteen and was not about to let someone tell me anything. I ignored him, hoping he would just walk away. He must have been feisty that evening because he didn't back down.

As his persistence manifested into anger, because I kept ignoring him, he began waving his right hand, which was holding his cigarette, in my face. He demanded I get up right that second and do the dishes.

I didn't like cigarette smoke and started waving it out of my face. I guess he took this as an act of aggression. He instantly grabbed my hair and drug me

14

through the den, the dining room, the kitchen, and downstairs towards my bedroom. I was kicking and screaming, begging him to let go as I clawed and tried to pry his powerful grip from my hair.

I kept begging him to let go. The harder I struggled to get away, the more my hair felt it was being ripped from my scalp. My ass hit each step as we made our way to my bedroom. He threw me on my bed.

"Is this what you want, you want me to put you in the hospital?" He yelled.

I had enough. I yelled back with all my might, "Yes, motherfucker! Go ahead and put me in the hospital."

At this point, all of the blame and hatred started to surface. I blamed my mom for my dad leaving when I was four, and now I was blaming the same father I desperately wanted to live with for all of those years for my current problems. Blame was something I learned at an early age, and I used it whenever it would benefit me for many years to come.

His girlfriend came downstairs and decided to offer her two cents. This was something my dad and I needed to figure out, but she insisted.

"See what you make your dad do? See how mad you make him? You are an ungrateful little shit, that is what you are!" She screamed.

The situation was only escalating, and all of my anger I could think of left my tongue with no reserve. I cussed, I yelled, I cried, and I let those two have it.

They stood there and allowed me to speak my mind then they both calmly left. Things changed that December night. The next day we had a conversation at the dinner table. I was informed I would no longer be going to my mom's every weekend but rather every other weekend. I would also have to walk to school, skipping any rides. I was not able to talk on the phone unless it was my mother and it had to be in front of either my dad or his girlfriend. I would also have to do chores for four hours each Saturday and Sunday that I was home.

I wasn't sure what to say. I was sad and angered by the position in which I found myself. I missed my friends from the school I left, I hated every minute that I was attending this other school, and I missed my grandma and playing sports. I was tired of being nice and feeling that everyone was a dick to me. I wanted to smoke weed again. I wanted to forget who I was. Every weekend that I went to mom's, that is what I did, I smoked pot when my mom was busy, and I forgot all of my troubles. Every other Sunday night when I went back to my dad's the prison mentality set back in – I felt oppressed.

Chapter 2
Departure to Freedom

Only a few months went by. April came very quickly. I was in Driver's Ed and set to get my driver's license soon. I was done with the driving part and was in no hurry because my dad said I would have to prove myself to get my license.

I was getting stoned every weekend I was at my mom's and, as far as I knew, neither my mom nor dad knew what I was doing. It worked for me. My mom would work late on Friday nights and go out afterward trying to find "true love." Hell, even Saturdays she would sometimes go out. My buddies and I would have the house all to ourselves and smoke joints, blunts, one-hitters, or even bongs. I was mad about everything. My grades were slipping, which was my fault. It made me horribly upset when I thought about them. The fact that my dad forgot to send in my IMSA (Illinois Math and Science Academy) paperwork made me furious. So to balance myself I continued shoving these dark thoughts in a pitch-black corner by smoking. But when you combine darkness with more darkness, all you are left with is darkness – flashlights cannot even guide the way.

April was about to become a month I would never forget. I was banned from being on the phone. One day after school, I answered the phone for whatever reason. It was my dad's girlfriend's mom. I told her they had not made it home from work yet, and I asked if she would like me to take a message. She politely said no and that she would just call back later.

My dad and his girlfriend got home from work around 5:00 p.m. We had dinner and everything was cleaned up by 6:00 p.m. I went to my room to listen to my radio – wishing I was anywhere but there. My dad had full custody, so it's not like I could just move out. I heard the phone ring. Within fifteen minutes, I heard the

17

footsteps. Being in the basement, I could always hear footsteps and could pick out whose they were – my sisters, my dad's girlfriend, etc. Like giant sledgehammers being dropped from the roof, I heard boom, boom, boom. That feeling you get in your chest when you are nervous, that fight or flight feeling, the feeling where your heart almost drops to the pit of your stomach, that is the impression that I had. I knew those footsteps – wishing with all of my might that I hadn't. They were angry footsteps of my father, but I wasn't sure what I did this time.

He hit that bottom step, his eyes bulged with determination, and every cuss word was spoken from the time he left the bottom step and ending up at the foot of my bed. He grabbed my pant leg and pulled me off the bed. I wasn't sure what he was mad about, but I quickly found out.

"You son of a bitch! I told you not to be on the phone. And you didn't even take a message!" He screamed.

"I thought it was you guys, you weren't home at your usual time. She said she would call back and that I didn't need to leave a message," I clamored.

"There is caller I.D. you liar."

"I just picked it up. I didn't check it."

He swung at me and missed; I swung back, my fist clenched; I missed. His girlfriend came downstairs to again provide her two cents like we were a charity. That was it. I wanted to leave.

"I want out of here. I don't wanna be here any fucking more," I pleaded as I started packing a heavy-duty black trash bag with my clothes.

"Fine, you want outta here, then you can leave. We will finally have some peace with you gone."

What hurt the most was his reassurance that I was a nuisance to everyone in the house. I did everything I could to let him know that his comment didn't bother me.

I packed my stuff, loaded it in the bed of his Chevy pickup, and we were off to my mom's.

I remember everything vividly from that truck ride. I was crying, "Hold the Line" by Toto was playing on the radio, and my dad had his aviators on with a stone-cold look on his face. We pulled up to my mom's. He put my stuff on her porch, asked for his house key back, and said that he was no longer my father.

"If we see each other in public, consider us strangers," he professed.

I was devastated to hear those words. My mom wasn't home, and I was left by myself. I couldn't quit crying. I cried so hard that I was having trouble breathing. I sat on the porch, dialing numbers where my mom might be, and I was finally able to get a hold of her.

I wanted to be back at the school I felt comfortable at. But I didn't want it to be at the expense of my dad.

My mom was a hairdresser, and she had my younger brother to worry about. She didn't make much money, and all I had was one hundred dollars in a bank account my grandma started for me. I went into my survival mode and couldn't wait to smoke some weed with my buddies.

My mom was at my aunt and uncle's house so she sent my uncle after me. He picked me up, knowing I needed a job. As we drove to his house, we talked about my options. He worked at IHOP and promised to speak with his boss the following day for me.

Everyone wanted to console me once we got to his house but I just wanted to play video games and forget about what was going on. I knew smoking weed would really help, but that would have to wait.

Just as he promised, my uncle called me the next day. I lived only a few blocks from IHOP so he suggested that I walk down there. I met with his boss, and she offered me a job. I had no other option. If I wanted to have what I thought were cool clothes or any spending money, I would have to take the job. I was officially a bus boy. The term bus boy is kind of demoralizing if you ask me. I wasn't a boy. I started telling people I was a table technician in good fun. It sounded a hell of a lot better than bus boy.

IHOP is where I would meet another great friend that I am still very close with today – Kevin. He and his friends would come into IHOP with baggy pants, black gloves, black eyeliner, and just a lot of black. It wasn't the mainstream fashion trend, but something was cool about these guys. They spoke about things that mattered. Kevin and I started talking in between the table cleaning, and he would see me walking to work, offering me a ride. Kevin and I would talk about life, dreams and goals we had, and how to prevent ourselves from conforming to the mainstream. But the guys I worked with showed me a different way of exploring.

I worked my butt off, smoked whenever I was off of work, and saved money whenever I could. This is where I met a twenty-something crowd I started hanging out with. Sixteen years old, I was earning a paycheck then I was invited to my first house party. I was skeptical at first. I didn't drink, and these guys were all about drinking and from the sound of it, partying pretty hard.

After work on a Friday night, I rode with the cook to his apartment. There were people already there as we walked in. I felt out of place. I still had my work clothes on with crusted-over pancake batter, and I knew I smelt like stale grease. He either smelt my fear, or it was written all over my face because he asked if I wanted to smoke. I typically liked to smoke alone or with a few people, but I went ahead and started passing a joint with some guy I never met as my friend from work went to the kitchen.

I saw my buddy walking back towards me with two beers in his hand. I kept telling myself I hope that second one isn't for me. Of course, he gave me a beer. I was afraid to tell him I had never drunk before. I opened the can and took a deep breath. I took my first drink. It was... it was... disgusting!

"You never drank before, have you?" the cook, my newly found buddy, asked.

"No," I replied.

I put the can back to my lips, and he tilted it from the bottom of the can, forcing me to drink faster. It was so gross. He witnessed my pain and pulled me into the kitchen.

"Here, this is probably more up your alley," he said as he handed me a soda mixed with whiskey. I took a drink, and the warm sensation was new, but I liked it. I liked the way it tasted. Thirty minutes went by, and my head felt clear, and the lights seemed brighter. I soon forgot about my pancake-battered work clothes and started laughing with everyone.

I didn't realize it, but I was again finding another way to deal with my insecurities and problems. It was awesome to be able to forget all the b.s. what I thought was everyone else's fault. I was free from my dad, free from worry, and I figured I found true freedom. Boy, was I wrong.

Chapter 3
The Day I Thought I Became a Man

I turned seventeen, and that is when I started hanging out with my other uncle and his friends. They were all twenty-one or older so getting served liquor was easily achieved when I was with them. The funny thing was that my uncle and his buddy worked at a liquor store – yes a liquor store. This worked out perfectly for me. I quit IHOP for another pancake joint for a pay increase and protection from a weakly-established union. The liquor store was right across the street.

I would take my lunch break and go visit my uncle or his buddy, who happened to work at the liquor store. I thought I was really something, being able to go in the store. I would go into the back cooler where my uncle was. In between stocking the shelves of wine coolers and cases of beer, he would be smoking bats, a pinch-hitter if you're not too sure of the lingo. He always told me the cold air would dilute the smell of the weed just like the cooks at IHOP. I am not certain if that is true, but he believed it.

He would always ask if I wanted a pinch-hit but I would never smoke if I was still working. When I got stoned, I would get really mellow and turned into what some may call a "poo brain."

It became an almost every weekend ordeal. My uncle's buddy needed money so he would sell me discounted beer and liquor. I would take fifty dollars into the store and walk out with three or four cases of beer, twp fifths of liquor, and a few half-pints of Schnapps for any girls that couldn't stand whiskey or bourbon.

I would have everyone calling me on Friday night at work or giving me their money on Thursday or Friday before we got out of school. I felt like I was somebody. I was still a virgin, but I was a virgin somebody!

My buddies, there were six of us who would hang

out regularly, kept giving me grief about being a prude. They would tell me all the time that I "weaked it" with this girl or that girl. Damn assholes wouldn't leave me alone about it. My best friend Justin was the worst. So what did I do? I started talking to a girl, with whom Justin was coordinating, to help me lose my cursed virginity.

Justin would be the messenger. He had a class with her more often and would always try to arrange for us to hang out.

Then one day… "Dude, dude," he yelled as he ran from the East Building trying to catch up to me, "she wants to do something with you. You're gonna get some."

"Whatever. Does she really?" I asked.

"Uh, yeah, well she calls it hang out but you know she gonna like the D."

"Whatever, you're an asshole. So when does she want to hang out?"

"She wants you to call her tonight to set something up," he said, handing me a piece of paper with her number.

I was nervous, unsure, and excited all at the same time. I had only kissed a couple of girls and had one "French handshake" up until this point in my life. I already developed in my mind that I was going to finally get some sex. I had not even called her yet.

I went home from school in a hurry. I had to work, so I wanted to call her before I left. When I dialed the phone, I would start with the first three numbers and hang up. I started laughing and shaking my head. "Just do it you sissy," I said to myself.

I dialed the whole number, it rang once, and then I hung up. "Aghh… you wuss, just call her."

I dialed it again, and it started ringing. My heart was pounding, and I was terrified of her answering for some reason. "Don't pick up, don't pick up, don't pick up," I kept repeating.

Then… she picked up.

"Hello?" she asked.

"Uhh… hi."

"Ty, is that you?"

"Haha, yes. Hey, I gotta go to work but, um… I wanted to call and see if you wanna do something this Friday."

"Sure. What do you wanna do?"

Holy crap, what did I wanna do? I couldn't answer that question honestly. I wasn't sure exactly what to say. My wingman wasn't around for me to consult with him.

"Hello, you there?"

"Haha, yes I am here. I was thinking maybe the arcade where the old 7-Eleven use to be." I said as that was the first thing I could think of instead of sounding like a pig and blurting out SEX.

"That sounds cool, wanna pick me up at 7?"

Wouldn't you know it, I didn't have a car and my mom's Mercury Sable was a POS. I wasn't sure what to tell her. "Uh… I don't have a car right now." I thought that was it. My chance to "hang out" with her was over, done, finished.

"That's okay, I'll come get ya. You live on Penning right?"

I was shocked again, what else did she know. "Yeah, that is correct."

"I'll be there at 7… Oh, and you can call me tonight when you get off if you want."

"Sure, talk tonight," I said as I hung up the phone. I was excited and smiling ear to ear. I went to work and couldn't wait to get off so we could talk.

It took forever for ten o'clock to come around. But once it was, I punched my time card, and I ran home – full steam. I lived pretty close to this job too so it only took a few minutes to get there.

I ran inside, I grabbed the phone, and I dialed. She answered, and we talked for nearly two hours about nothing. I did my best to try and be cool, but I was nervous the whole time. When we first started talking, I kept thinking to myself sex, but the more we talked, the more I forgot about that. We ended our phone call as we told each other good night. I went to bed wishing it was 7 o'clock on Friday; I really wanted to see her.

The next two days felt like a week. But finally, Friday had come. The bell rang, and I did not have to be back at school until Monday morning and come Monday I would return to school after my final metamorphosis. I would return... a man.

Justin and I got a ride to my house. He was just about as excited as I was. About four hours before she would be picking me up, I was already figuring out what I could wear that would impress her. I wasn't trying on a bunch of "outfits," but I needed to impress her. I lived in a house I was not thankful for and in all honesty quite embarrassed by, and she was picking me up.

Thoughts kept running through my head about stories I have heard of some guys' first times, and some were stories I wouldn't want to be repeated. Time wasn't on their side, to say the least. If my heart could have, it would have jumped out of my chest from beating so hard. I wasn't even on the date yet, and I was already predicting what was going to happen. I was VERY optimistic.

Before I knew it, it was time. Justin was stoned out of his mind. I didn't want to smoke yet because I would become "poo brain." When I would smoke and get my brain all relaxed and lazy, my sense of humor made no sense to anyone other than someone that was stoned. So to save myself from any unwanted embarrassment, I passed on smoking till later.

I looked at the clock, 7:01 pm. She was late. I thought she was going to stand me up then... a honk. I thought I was nervous for the past four hours; it felt like my heart belly flopped into my stomach once I heard that honk.

I opened the front door and signaled to her "just a minute." I looked at Justin, his eyes looking like the Red Sea, and asked if he wanted to go. He agreed.

When I told her he was going, she was cool with it then we drove to the little arcade.

Justin kept to himself, playing video games so she and I could hang out. We hit it off. We couldn't keep our hands off of each other. Justin kept looking at me with his slanted eyes. He knew I was nervous beyond belief. We left after about two hours of being there, and it couldn't have been soon enough.

We returned to my house, and it was just as empty as the night the first time I smoked the hijacked weed I took from my grandma. Mom would be out until at least 1 a.m., and my brother was with his dad. Each step I took towards the house came along with deep breaths. I did my best to hide my anxiety.

Once we got into the living room Justin handed me a condom right in front of her. My face became hot and probably redder than a lobster. He smiled from ear to ear, and she took my hand guiding me towards the back of the house where my bedroom was.

"Which room?" she asked.

My throat was incapable of answering her without cracking like I was going through puberty all over again. "Right there," I screeched as I pointed to my bedroom.

It was really going to happen. I really started to panic. She began kissing me and directing my hand better than Stanley Kubrick. She told me to turn off the light. The moonlight slightly broke through my window as I watched her remove her shirt, pants, and then she laid down on my bed. She signaled me to come over to her.

As silly as this seems, I kept thinking of the line from "Beavis and Butthead" when Butthead would say, "Come to Butthead."

But, back to my rite of passage.

I removed my pants and approached her. I would say 1.37 minutes later, I was changed. I heard Handel's Messiah, "Hallelujah…Hallelujah…Hallelujah" playing in my mind.

She kissed me when we were done. I flipped on the lights, and we got dressed. I felt amazing. The feeling during and after was just as great as getting high or drunk. I wasn't thinking about anything. A smile overtook my face.

We walked out to the living and Justin, and my other buddy were sitting there. They started clapping. She and I both started smiling as I shook my head. I walked her to her car. We talked for about ten minutes, and she left. I couldn't wait to talk to her again.

I was in love. I always wanted to be with her. The first two months were great. Then the last month of our relationship was horrible. I could only imagine on her part. I was a very jealous and insecure individual.

Now some of you might be wondering why I would include this is. There is very good reason. It was a big part of my life, and I am setting myself up for distraction after distraction. I put in the intro that priorities are crucial. Mine, as you can see, are very misguided.

Without my grandma, my dad's mom, around, or my father, my mother and I were always fighting. I was always checking on my girlfriend. I would call her and always want to know where she was at and what she was doing. A lot of this had to do with my first girlfriend in seventh grade. I know some of you may not remember what being in love in seventh grade is like, but I really liked the first girl I called an actual girlfriend. We dated for almost nine months, and that is a damn long time to a thirteen-year-old. My girlfriend in seventh grade gave me the cold shoulder after those nine months. She broke up with me with what would be equivalent to a text – a handwritten note to be passed to me by her friend. So with my girlfriend that I gave my special moment to, I remembered what happened to me in seventh grade. I did everything I could to prevent that from happening. But, after three long months of the best relationship I had ever had up until that moment, she left me. She gave me the cold shoulder.

I was crushed. I couldn't look at her pictures so Justin and I burned them on my front porch. I felt dead inside. The only way I knew how to make that horrible feeling go away was to smoke and drink.

That is what I did. I kept working, partying, and reliving this every day. In a world where I used to be optimistic, I was slowly becoming bitter – especially towards women. Through all of these moments leading up to this time in my life, I finally had the tools to build a wall. And like Steven Tyler of Aerosmith said, "kept the right ones out and let the wrong ones in. Had an angel of mercy to see me through all my sins. There were times in my life when I was going insane, trying to walk through the pain." The only way I could shelter myself from the realities of the world was through sex, drugs, and some bad-ass rock-n-roll, literally. I listened to bands like Korn, Limp Bizkit, Deftones, Rage Against the Machine, Slipknot, Soulfly and much more.

The inception of my insidious attitude now grew ten feet tall. The fun was only about to begin.

Chapter 4

Freedom to Departure Part II

Before we continue, so we are very clear, what is written in the previous chapter is not intended to scorn or diminish the girl I lost my virginity too. She was and still is an excellent human being. I have no reason to explain myself but for the sake of explaining myself, I included the relationship I had, not just to a girl but to a defining moment in my life that is a reality. I used this as a way to further blame the world and everyone in it for my problems. My heart was broken when she didn't want to be with me any longer. After about a month, I moved on but the hate and anger did not. She didn't create this hate, the way I did. In a day and age where our sensitivity seems to reign supreme, I want you to ask yourself if you would like to keep reading. It is going to get more interesting, to say the least. If you want to avoid the truth that happened in my life then I would close this book or close the app you are reading from – you are free to choose.

Now that we got that out of the way let us continue.

My mother and I were constantly fighting. I was keeping my grades at a C average minimum. I ended up getting my first F. When I had seen the F on my progress report, my first thought was that people were going to think I was stupid. It wasn't a thought of, "Oh, I better pick up the slack."

My mom and I couldn't get along. My friends and I took over her house even though she wasn't there very often. I worked hard and played even harder. I was no longer a boy. I lost my virginity and provided for myself. I had no one to tell me what to do. So when my mom would try to run her home, I thought she was only trying to control what I was doing in my life; I didn't think she had the right. I couldn't tell you how many days we spent screaming in each others' faces. She would always throw in my face I would never talk to my dad or grandma the way I spoke to her. She was right. But I would rebuttal, reminding her that they would never treat me the way that she did. I was a big smart ass. It was a constant push and pull. My mother was, at the time, doing her best and I did everything in my power to remind her that it wasn't good enough. I was never physical, but I was quite verbal. I couldn't tell you how many times we would both be frothing at the mouth and I would storm out of the house angrier than I was the day before. I would walk from our house to my grandpa's, talking to myself, blaming anyone I could think of for my situation. What would take twenty minutes of walking to get to his house felt like only a few minutes. I couldn't stand living with my mom anymore. I was just biding my time until graduation.

I met a girl that I liked in school. I had my neighbor from across the street pass notes to her, and like Justin did, she coordinated with this girl to meet at one of our school's football games. I was always shy when it came to a girl that I liked. This girl was always smiling when I would see her in the halls. When we met by the East Building that Friday night, I wasn't sure what to say. She was in the band, and it intrigued me even more that she played the saxophone. I wanted to know everything about her. So I asked her for her number, and we started talking every night. I would call her on my break at work, and then we finally decided to do something. It was about a month of talking before we committed to a date. Soon after the date began, we did our "thing". We did our thing so much over the course of the next few weeks that putting the prophylactics in the trash was getting to be dangerous, risking my mom finding out. What did I do to solve this dilemma? I started flushing them.

One weeknight, I came home from work around 10:30 p.m. As I walked through the front door the computer screen lightly glowed. It was unusual because my mom typically had the computer turned off. It caught my attention as I squinted and glared at the computer screen. I could see an outline of a piece of paper. I looked at the paper once I got close enough to read and it said, "We need to talk. –Mom". We usually did not have talks; we usually had an argument of built up frustrations.

I walked to her bedroom door and lightly tapped on it.

"You awake?" I asked.

She cleared her throat and replied, "Yes I am. So have you been downstairs?"

I wasn't sure why she would ask this. I thought she might have found some weed that one of my buddies or I might have stashed down there and forgotten all about. "Nooooo, why?" I said as I laughed.

Even though we didn't get along, I didn't want her to know I was smoking weed or drinking quite a bit. She found Marlboro Reds in my book bag once, and I told her I was holding it for a friend and I think she believed me. She never confiscated the cigarettes, so I guess we will never know.

"Go down there and look," she ordered.

I didn't ask questions so I went to our basement. She had left the light on intentionally so I would be able to see what she wanted to talk about. I made my way down to the last step and stopped. There was about a foot or so of standing water. My first thought was, "Why does she want me to see the water. I didn't do this." Then I investigated the water with more of my attention, and there they were - a whole community of rubbers floating like they were lost at sea. I started busting up laughing. I didn't know what else to do. It was so funny; I didn't even want to try and blame it on Justin or another one of my buddies.

I made my way back to mom's room, laughing hysterically.

"It's not funny Ty," she said trying not to laugh, "this is my house, and I didn't think your girlfriend was like that."

I turned on my mom's bedroom light, and she couldn't help but laugh.

"Mom, we are at that age," I said with tears of laughter falling from my eyes.

She tried so hard to turn her smile into a scorned facial expression, but she had no luck. "At least you're being safe and don't DO IT on my bed."

"Too late for that mom, good night," I said as I ran to my bedroom.

"What!" I heard her scream as I shut my door laughing.

I started hanging out with my girlfriend more often and my buddies less. We would make sure to hang out every once in a while but for almost the first year of dating, I would only hang out with them once a week if that. They would always call me a pussy or something. I didn't care. I thought I was in love.

It was spring of my senior year, and graduation was right around the corner. I started to miss hanging out with my buddies. The novelty of being "in love" was wearing off, and I started hanging out with them more often and her less. One of the thoughts I had was that I was going to be in college, and I couldn't have an anchor weighing me down. We were a year and a half apart in age so she was still going to be in high school. It started getting sour between her and me. I couldn't just break up with her because the thought of her being with another guy was unacceptable to me. I wasn't sure what to do so instead of forcing myself to be alone, I kept dating her.

I started hanging out with other girls. My buddies and I would go to parties where my girlfriend wasn't, and I would get stoned and liquored up. I would find a girl to mess around with. It was always easier for me when booze and pot were involved. I would always tell my girlfriend I would come over and meet her to hang out, but I knew I would go out and be unfaithful. I did this intentionally to control her. I didn't want her to find another person because I knew I was being horrible. She offered comfort when I needed it. I used her whenever I could. If she tried questioning my motives, I would never get physical, but I did get verbal.

Graduation came, and we continued to date. I went to college and continued on with my charades. I lied day after day but continued to string her along.

Before starting school, my mom and I went to a "Buy Here Pay Here" and I financed my first car – a Chrysler LeBaron convertible. I thought it was kind of a "girly" car, but it was mine. I was paying for it. I didn't know any better. The interest rate was around the twenty-seven percent range, but I didn't know the difference or even what a good interest rate was. It was red with a few scratches, but it was perfect. I was starting to feel like an actual adult.

After my first semester at Lewis and Clark Community College, I wanted a more adult job. I reached out to my cousin. Her mom and step dad owned a cell phone store. I informally applied and started working at one of their locations. I was making more per hour than I was at the Pancake Ranch, plus I was making a commission on top of my hourly. With a car and a good-paying, "respectable" job, my ego started getting way out of control.

I would ignore my girlfriend regularly. My mom and I were not fighting as often because I was busy with school and work. My cousin, who helped get me get the job at the cell phone store, wanted to get a place together. It was time to finally move on. My younger brother was older and needed his own room, and I was tired of looking at the house. My cousin and I found a home and gave the property owners an application. We had my cousin's mom co-sign on the application and without any complications, we were approved.

I would have a whole finished basement to myself,

and she and her young son would have the entire upstairs. I had credit cards, a decent amount in my bank account, paid all of my bills on time, and moved into this house a free man. I had only one problem, I thought – my girlfriend. It was getting harder on the both of us as I would usually ignore her. We finally broke up for the first time. She was completely devastated, and I wasn't even sure why. I was a complete jerk.

I started having house parties and all of my friends, and their friends would come over. We were an every weekend hang out spot. We had a dart board, good stereo, and a card table. Things would get crazy. One night I caught someone snorting cocaine. At this time in my life, I only agreed with pot and alcohol. I told them that they can go to their car and come back if they wanted. My ex-girlfriend would always call and want to talk and set a date to hang out. Even though we weren't dating, I would still try to hang out with her and keep her away from other guys. So I started with making promises that I never kept.

Things were going great; I just got health, dental, and vision insurance through work. I just purchased a new Honda Civic, added subs, and a new radio. I wasn't really doing great in college in all of my classes, but I was working and making good money for a college student.

My cousin and I started butting heads over the silliest things. She kept using my hair brush, and I would get furious. I would get mad about the dirty kitchen. Our year lease was up so we parted ways because she wanted to buy a house. A friend I worked with at the cell phone store was going to SIUE and wanted to get a townhouse apartment in Edwardsville, so we did. It was more expensive than the house with my cousin and farther from my college, but it was right in SIUE college town. Our first thought was all the girls we could have over to our house parties. We started having the girls' softball team, his friends, and my friends all come over. We had a packed party almost every weekend for about two months. It was getting old for him, my drinking was all of the time, and I only smoked weed every once in a while. It turned into a paranoia session when I would smoke. We started butting heads. He was tired of the people over all of the time, and I was going broke. From my car payment, rent, and my credit card minimums, I had to abandon ship. I just left him with the rent – no explanation. He eventually was let out of the lease and took off on his own personal adventure to Colorado.

What was funny is my dad, and I started talking again in the midst of all of the newly generated chaos. He left his girlfriend that I couldn't stand and said I could live with him and grandma again, if I wanted to, so I did.

Moving back in with my dad was strange. I was out on my own for almost three years and had a tremendous amount of parties, but now I was back at a calm house. My grandma was staying at my aunt's in North Carolina for a few months, so it was just my dad and me. My ex-girlfriend I had treated horribly got back with me for a few months before my twenty-first birthday.

I was still working, making significant money, and had to get my wisdom teeth pulled. I was able to use my dental insurance and had them removed at our family dentist I had used since I was a little kid. After they had been removed, I was prescribed hydrocodone or better known as Vicodin. They only prescribed twenty because the office manager said that is all I should need. I had my girlfriend drive me home, and the pain was something stupid. The holes in my gums were packed with gauze, and my mouth was throbbing. When I got home, I read the bottle, and it said to take one to two every four or six hours. I was hurting pretty bad, so I decided to take two. My girlfriend and I were sitting there talking; then fifteen minutes later after taking the pills a feeling came over me, a feeling almost better than sex, getting stoned, or getting drunk. I felt amazing. My head was lighter than it has ever been and I didn't have a care in the world. I wasn't thinking about being cool enough or wearing the right clothes or driving the coolest car. And I was actually talking with my girlfriend without being an asshole. I found the cure to my unhappiness and all of my insecurities and worries. Pandora's Box was discovered that day, or so I thought.

Chapter 5
On Top of the World

After taking the legally-prescribed enlightenment in a pill, I never thought any harm would come from them. At this point in my life, I was doing pretty well. I was almost finished with getting my Associate's Degree, which was taking longer than it should have. Coincidentally, I ran into an old friend I had not seen in a while. We started talking about this and that, and it somehow led to the topic of the little white miracle pills, Vicodin.

He continued to tell me that I could buy them on the streets because people were selling their prescriptions to make money, whether it was for their bills or to buy other drugs like crack cocaine. What did I do? I started buying just a few. That is how it starts – a few here and there.

My girlfriend and I were not doing too well. I was back to my old tricks and needed "my space." We became real distant again. I happened to take a plane ride out to North Carolina to visit my grandma and other family because my cousin was finally getting married. I took a week vacation to spend time with everyone, drink beer by the in-ground pool (I thought I was really cool), and attend his wedding. I actually felt cool because my aunt and uncle were pretty successful people. They owned a buffet style restaurant, so they had a beautiful house in a neighborhood, which had, I believe, a Home Owner's Association. They had to keep their grass cut to a certain length, and they were forced to change their privacy fence because it was the wrong color of white.

After I had flown home from my cousin's wedding, the first thing I did was I drove to my dad's brother's house, to see how he was doing. I had two more days before Monday came and I had to be back at work. While we were standing outside talking, a girl, a beautiful goddess of a girl, came walking out of the house directly next to his. Her hair was dark and a little bit past her shoulders. Her eyes were hazel and almost sparkled in the sun, forcing me into some type of seduced trance. As I stood there on the sidewalk, he signaled her over so that he may introduce us. As she approached closer, time started to slow down, and I was mesmerized by practically everything.

"Hey, this is my nephew," he said.

I felt it. All of a sudden I was getting "poo" brain. I had not smoked, drank, or took a pill that day but just being in the presence of her made me all blah in a good way.

"Hey, my name is Christina," she said as she tucked a strand of hair behind her ear.

I stared at her and smiled not knowing what to say on account of my "poo" brain. I kept thinking, "Say something idiot, she is going to believe you are stupid."

"Hey, how are you?" I asked.

She tucked another strand of hair neatly behind her other ear as she smiled, looked to the ground, and said, "Fine."

I wasn't sure what was going on. At this point in my life, with or without drugs or alcohol, I was pretty good at talking to girls but with her it was difficult.

"She is sisters with your cousin's girlfriend from Bunker Hill," my uncle informed me.

I knew her sister. She was pretty cool.

I ended up leaving without any type of conversation. I knew she thought I was a jerk. But wouldn't you know it, the next day as I was filing away some customer contracts at work, my phone started to ring. I looked down at my cell but wasn't familiar with the number.

"Hello?"

"What's going on stud," an unfamiliar girl's voice said.

Slightly confused I answered with a question, "Fine, who is this?"

"It's Julia, Christina's sister that you met yesterday."

"Yeah, well your sister is gorgeous. So what's up?"

You could hear her laughing, and I started to get confused. "Hey, well, since you think my sister is gorgeous, and she thinks you are hot, would you want to do something with her?"

A girl thought I was hot. My ego began to flex, and my inner "playa" started to surface. It was almost like a magical incantation was spoken, transforming me into a smooth, confident, stud (as Christina's sister said.)

WARNING: This part may make you sick to your stomach.

"She thinks I'm hot, huh? Well, Julia, what does she want to do?" I asked.

"I dunno, for you to call her first. Then maybe go out. Her and her boyfriend, who is a mighty douche bag, just broke up recently so she is ready to do something."

"Mmmkay, I see. I got ya. Well, I have a date this Friday, but I could cancel it for her if she wants to hang out."

Julia started to laugh. "You don't have a date plus don't be treating her like all the other girls."

Startled that she would suggest that I would treat a girl badly, I asked, "What do you mean the other girls?"

"Ty, come on, you do have a rep for sleeping with them and not talking to them again."

"Nah, I don't do that," I said as I laughed, "Okay, well I promise I won't do that to her."

Julia reminded me to call her and set things up to hang out so that is just what I did. I called Christina when I got home from work, and we talked for a little bit. She was pretty cool, she was going to college too, liked video games, and sounded sexier than hell on the phone. I kept thinking of her eyes, smile, and laugh. I really dug this girl but wait, what about my current sort-of girlfriend. I have never actually liked another girl since we have been dating on and off.

Christina and I talked Monday, Tuesday,

Wednesday, and Thursday. I asked her Thursday if she wanted to do something Friday and she agreed.

Friday came. As I drove up to Christina's house, I started to get nervous. The first date wasn't anything special. We were just going to go eat and play darts. Since I moved back in with my dad, he and I went to bars quite a bit to drink. I got kind of good at darts, so I wanted to flirt with her by beating her – weird I know.

I knocked on her door, and a little girl with glasses answered. She looked up, hit me in my stomach, smiled, and said, "Hi! You must be the hot guy here for my sister. She's downstairs."

I walked into their house, which was complete insanity. A young little boy was cradling his knees in the corner by the stairs crying. Kids were running upstairs back and forth, screaming. I suddenly had red lights flashing in my head to leave while I still had a chance. Then I heard two adults screaming at one another. I felt very uncomfortable until "she" looked up at me from the basement steps.

"Come down here," she said as my heart skipped a few beats from the excitement.

"K," I said walking down the steps as I saw a beer in her hand. Instantly, I was turned off. I didn't think she should be drinking yet. I was strange, I know. I also hated when girls would let cigarettes hang out of the corner of their mouths and talk at the same time. But I did not let this distract me entirely from our date. I sat around waiting for her to get ready.

Finally, we made it to the bar and grill. Dinner came quickly and so did the drinks. I wasn't taking pills on a daily basis quite yet so our first date was only alcohol.

I kept ordering my 7 & 7 and her beer. She was an excellent kisser. I couldn't keep my hands off of her. I kept beating her in darts, and she was getting mad – very competitive and I liked it. We kept kissing in between throws and decided to go back to her place to "watch" a movie and chill (equivalent to Netflix & Chill). We made it back to her house and the two adults that were fighting when I picked her up were still arguing. We made our way to her bedroom, closed the door, and locked it.

As some of you may think, we did not do "our" thing. That would happen in two weeks from this night. We made out, stared into each others' eyes, and made out some more. I felt so comfortable, I fell asleep.

The following morning I woke up to wearing my same clothes and her staring at me with her beautiful eyes as she sat on her knees on her bed, where I slept all night. I wasn't sure what the look was for, but I still liked her in the morning, and we didn't even have sex.

Once we had sex, it was an everyday thing. I somehow managed to keep this all a secret from my current girlfriend until someone that we mutually knew told her. I told this guy with the expectation he would uphold the guy code and keep his mouth quiet, but he didn't. He went to my current ex-girlfriend/girlfriend and told her how I told him about the scratches on my back and other "dirty" details. I was still stringing her along though we were not technically dating any longer. But as I would find out, if you still have feelings for someone you are still vulnerable.

My current ex-girlfriend/girlfriend, soon to be officially my ex again, came to my house after finding out my recent excursions. She stood in front of me with her look of heartbreak, tears pouring down her face. She had only one question for me, "Why Ty, why?"

I looked at her and suddenly started to feel guilty, ashamed, and downright horrible for what I did to her. I didn't love her anymore, but I didn't feel right for what I had done.

"You could have just let me go, told me no more," she screamed, "instead, I found out from Josh."

I stood there blank faced and about to cry. I wasn't

sure how to handle the situation so what did I do? I started blaming her.

"It's your fault, constantly calling me, you won't leave me alone. We are not even technically together," I stupidly spewed from my mouth.

Her tears accelerated, and all she could do was shake her head, get in her car, and drive away.

I stood in my rocked driveway and watched her tail lights fade into the distance. I knew it was completely over; I had hurt her for the very last time. The really crappy thing was that I was okay with it despite feeling like a total dick. I had something to keep me distracted – a new girl, alcohol, and pills.

I left only a few minutes after she did and headed straight to my new girlfriend's house.

I had a good job, enough money to buy almost whatever I wanted, now that I had moved in with my dad, and had a new and beautiful girlfriend I couldn't quit thinking of. I was on top of the world. But I was soon to find out that when you are at the top, sometimes, the only direction you can go is down.

Chapter 6

I Am In Control

Things were going spectacularly. Christina and I were getting along and hanging out quite a bit. Every minute I was not working or at school, we were together. Then one night she stayed with me at my grandma's house. My grandma, my dad's mom, was home and let me tell you that she was old school. Grandma was already in bed when we got there. We quietly came in and made my way to my bed. We started doing our "thing" and we were probably a little too loud.

The following day I took her home and came back. My grandma never really said much about the situation, but I knew that she knew what we did. We sat and talked for about twenty minutes and she told me that I would have to start paying rent and Christina could not stay the night any longer unless we were to get married.

I was so used to doing what I wanted when I wanted, I instantly got upset. My face began to get red but this was my grandma, and I was not about to start smarting off to her. So I did the next best thing I could think of... I called Christina, and I moved in with her. You see, her father left their mother, and she pretty much got to run the house.

My grandma and I still talked but never spoke of the situation again.

After a few months had gone by living with my girlfriend, I found out that a few members of her family were legally prescribed Vicodin. It was a win-win for me.

At this time, we had been dating for about six months, and I was getting a few pain pills from her family members here and there. I wasn't spending much on them, but I was taking anywhere from six to ten a week. I really liked taking them when I was at work. I felt I could sell anything to anybody.

Around the six month mark, things started getting

complicated. And if you have noticed anything in the timeline of this book, it's that I would usually abandon ship when things got a little tough or uncomfortable.

Christina's family kept going into her bedroom and taking whatever they wanted – clothes, jewelry, etc. I cared a lot about her, and since it made her upset, I started to do my best to protect her. I bought a lock for the door. They still managed to get into the bedroom. I purchased another lock and then left a note on the door. They still managed to get in.

Then one day, the day I feared would come, the ex-boyfriend showed up. Christina would be nice and go talk to him outside. Because of the friction between her family and me, they quit letting me have any Vicodin. This really pissed me off.

Another thing that really pissed me off was that her ex that she was with for quite a few years, and that happened to live with her too before they split up, was back on her doorstep like a stray cat begging for food and water. He would come at all times of the night knocking on the door begging for forgiveness.

I finally met my breaking point with this guy. I told Christina I wanted him to quit coming over. Her mom would let him in, and God only knows what her mom was telling him, as she didn't like me because of the lock, the notes, and my smart ass mouth.

I finally confronted him – face to face. I cannot remember the exact words we exchanged, but they were not pretty. I am not much of a fighter, but move in on what I think is my territory, and I don't back down.

Things started getting weird. He would not fight me. He would say all types of things that my friends and I would have called "douche-bag" slang. He wasn't a very good-looking guy, and he would always throw his arms up in the air – calling me out. I would walk towards him but every time I did he would back up, flip me the bird, and get in his truck and peel out. I can't help but picture a

Discovery Channel film crew filming this and turning the behaviors of the ex into a documentary.

I understood his pain, he liked her and what wasn't there to like? Christina was and still is stunning, funny, and awesome.

Around the year mark of our relationship, I was taking Vicodin, on average, a few days a week with the same amount. Christina and I were drinking every weekend and having an okay time. Her ex would not quit calling, coming around, or harassing her. I found out around this time that he was trying to be a cop. This guy was one of those fellows that should never, ever, be allowed to carry a badge and a gun. Today, he is a cop with a family, and all I can do is wish him the best.

Christina started to want her space. She wanted to think things over and wasn't quite sure what to do. Damn it. I had been there before. The girl that I liked a lot and gave my virginity to started doing the same exact thing. I started getting jealous and curious where she was when she didn't want to hang out. I bought her a phone and told her I expected her to answer it if I was going to pay the bill.

Instincts of mine started to kick in. If she wanted to play this game then fine, I knew I was pretty good at it. It was hard, though, I actually cared about her so one of the ways I dealt with it was to drink, take a few pills, smoke some weed, get paranoid, and hang out with my friends I didn't get to see that often.

The strain on our relationship started taking a toll. I traded my Honda Civic in for a new Nissan Frontier, and she told me that I should have talked to her about it before committing to a lengthier car loan. I was kind of shocked when she told me this. I say this detail because my attitude of "I don't answer to anybody" kicked in. So I let her say what she had to say as I reminded her it was my money and I worked for it.

It wasn't too long after I bought the truck that

Christina and her family moved. Her dad wasn't talking to me anymore because of my mouth and I heard through the grapevine Christina's mom kept trying to get her to leave me along with some of her friends. Her ex was still trying to call her and come around when I wasn't there.

Then in the midst of all of this insanity, my grandma fell ill. She was going in and out of the hospital for reasons I am still not sure of to this day. I moved back in with my dad and grandma. Christina didn't like it and we would go back and forth with dating. I started taking pills more often because my younger sister was able to get them on a regular basis. I was happy no more.

I finished Lewis and Clark and got my Associates Degree. I signed up to continue my education at SIUE to earn my Bachelor's Degree which did not last very long. Christina and I were still seeing each other and sleeping with one another but our relationship was toxic.

My younger sister always had friends over and I went out of my way to talk to these friends when Christina and I would break up and be mad at one another. One of my sister's friends, in particular, always helped me forget my heartache. I truly mean heartache. I wanted Christina and I to get along, share a bank account, and build great memories but either I was too stupid or we were too young. My sister's friend was funny and had a goofy, carefree attitude and she smoked, drank, and took some pills here and there.

Christina would yell at me to quit taking the pills, stop drinking so much, and whatever else she was trying to prevent me from doing that was destroying my life. Ahh, but this girl didn't care. She would sit next to me and pass a joint. It was bliss. I would go two to three days without talking to Christina. She was calling me daily and nightly. I would only return the call if I wasn't with this new girl. Again, do you see the pattern? Things get a little tough and what do I do?

My grandma's illness got worse. She was now at

home and refused to go back to the hospital any longer. My aunt moved in and helped tend to her. We had a hospital bed moved into the house and we all pitched in helping my grandma somehow and someway.

I have a relatively large family on both sides, but an even larger one on my dad's. People were showing up weekly. My family from out of town started flying or driving in. I didn't realize it was that serious, but it was. Christina and I hadn't talked for about a week or so then I got the call while I was at work. It was a Wednesday. One of my aunts said that Grandma Bechel probably wouldn't make it much longer. I tried to distract myself with work and pills, but it wasn't working. That gut wrenching feeling you get when something terrible is about to happen or did just happen took over my body.

My manager told me to go home after she witnessed the pale look on my face. I got there at soon as I could. My family filled our house. No one was really laughing and everyone stared into their distant reality, begging that this wouldn't happen. See, my grandma birthed seven children, one passed away at birth, and she helped raise my grandpa's three boys from his previous marriage. Cousins, uncles, aunts, nephews, and friends filled our house.

I walked into my grandma's room and there she was motionless except for her shallow breaths her body was somehow managing to take. The death rattle had begun mere minutes before I got there. My aunt had taped gauze over grandma's eyes to allow them to stay closed. I couldn't take it and for some reason all of the things I had done to her, my past girlfriends, friends, my mom, my dad, all began to surface as I was forced to witness a life complete its cycle.

I walked towards grandma's bed. The guard rails were up as I reached for her hand. They were getting cold so I took both of my hands and covered them. I could feel the knots of arthritis in her bones. A life of caring, hard work, and spoken lessons were fleeting her body. Slowly she was leaving but it was as if she wanted to say goodbye to everyone first. I rubbed her hands and apologized for everything. I was in the room by myself and I confessed my struggles and my mistakes. I begged her to stay. She was the only one that could help me understand myself and this mad world I lived in.

"Grandma, I am sorry," as tears rolled down my face.

I wanted her to say something, anything. I placed my head upon the steel rail, gripping her hand tightly with both of mine, and I wept.

"Grandma, I am losing interest in life, and if you go, I don't know what I will do. I treated you badly, I treated girls wrong, I treated mom badly, and dad I purposely tried making his life a living hell."

The room was quiet. A faint sound could be heard from the metal drawstring hitting the glass on the ceiling fan.

I didn't want to get up and leave grandma's side, but I had to; many more family members wanted to say their goodbyes.

I went into the back bedroom to sit on the couch. I was up for almost twenty-four hours as my we were anticipating my grandma's passing. It was hard for me to hold my eyes open then I dozed off.

I woke to my sister's boyfriend shaking me by my shoulder.

"Hey… hey… wake up man," he said quickly, "she's almost gone."

I sat up from the couch and made my way back to my grandma's room. It was jam packed with my family right by her side. I stood there, and I watched her lungs take her last deep breaths of life. Then… one of my cousins bellowed a sound of heartbreak, a sound I will never forget. As I type these words for whoever is reading this, tears are rolling down my face just like the day she left us. That day we all wept. The house grew silent of needless chatter, and all that could be heard were moans of pain and sobs of sadness. If you listened close enough, you probably could have heard tears hit the floor because they were just that heavy that day.

We all agreed not to call the coroner yet. We all wanted to say goodbye one last time. My aunt removed the gauze from grandma's eyes and she looked peaceful. We all stood in line, some of us kissed her like I did on her forehead and some of us cried so heavily that we couldn't breathe.

Three hours went by and we called the coroner to come get her. They came in and asked a few questions, took all of her medication, and placed her on the gurney. They rolled her through the kitchen to the living room and out the deck door. It all felt like a bad dream. Some of my family drank. Some of them smoked cigarette after cigarette. We all knew there was no turning back, and she was gone. I was worn out from crying and the lack of sleep so I went to bed.

I didn't talk with Christina for two days after grandma's passing until she called me.

"Hello," I said.

"I am so sorry about your grandma," Christina sympathetically told me.

She knew my pain of losing someone you care deeply for. Her sister who introduced us passed away in a car wreck a few months before grandma left.

"It's okay, thanks for calling. How are you?"

"I am okay. I have really needed to talk with you for two weeks or so but with your grandma and you don't act like you really wanna talk, I was putting it off."

"About what?"

"Well... uh hmm..."

"Come on spit it out."

She got quiet. I wasn't able to tell if she was still on the phone until she answered with something that left me speechless.

"Ty, I am not sure how to tell you this and now probably isn't the right time, but I'm pregnant."

Chapter 7
It Ain't Mine

"Pregnant? This cannot be right. There is no way in hell I can be a father," I thought to myself as I sat quietly listening to Christina's heavy breathing while she was waiting for me to say something to her.

I could only imagine a woman's thought when she unexpectedly finds out she is carrying the most precious creation humans are tasked with to complete – another life. Nine months of another living creature growing, moving, and learning right within their womb. At the time I didn't think that way at all.

"Are you sure it's mine?" I asked with a cocky tone like everything was her fault.

She was quiet for a second then it sounded like she was crying as she had begun to sniffle.

"You're an asshole... How fucking dare you!" She screamed followed by her hanging up the phone.

I sat there – thinking. I couldn't believe what I had just heard. I knew I wasn't ready to be a father. Being a father would mean taking responsibility, and the alcohol and pills were responsibility enough.

After a few days of thinking it over, I called Christina. We talked about it, and she still seemed angry. She told me she only wanted me to know and that she would take care of everything herself.

I was still seeing my sister's friend on the side and selfishly I thought about how much of a jerk I would look like.

I cared about Christina, but if I wanted to be with her that meant I would have to go to doctor visits, start sharing my money with her, and couldn't run around and do what I wanted. At the time it didn't seem like it was worth it. I even had thoughts that she could handle it herself. She was already complaining about me taking so many pills, and that would create more problems because

I didn't want to quit. I was a man, right? I worked and bought what I wanted, right? I thought this way and wasn't about to let her tell me how to live my life. It was easier to string her along just enough so I didn't become completely attached that I would compromise my lifestyle.

It eventually got so bad that I just quit going over to Christina's house. We stopped talking, and I was able to do what I wanted when I wanted. What I was really doing is running away, and this was something I had perfected as an art.

My sister's friend and I started hanging out more often. We would smoke weed, take pills frequently, and drink every once in a while. The pills were starting to take a front seat to everything else. My sister's friend would stay the night with me all of the time. My dad was finally having enough of her there. I would go to work, and she would stay at my house all day and practically do nothing except smoke cigarettes and weed. He asked that she stay at her house more often. Now, you have read enough, and you can probably predict what I am about to do here, if not, pay close attention.

I was pissed my dad would tell me what to do. What did I do? She and I moved in with her grandma. We stayed in a little room with a twin-sized bed. Her grandma was in for a rude awakening when it came to me and my attitude.

A couple of months went by, and my new girlfriend and I took over her grandma's house. We came and went when we pleased, made messes and half ass cleaned them up. The least I could have done being that I was staying there rent free was to mow the lawn maybe and clean up a little bit. That didn't happen. I was spending most of my money on pills and whatever was left over was for my truck, insurance, and cell phone bill.

Through my self-induced pill coma, the time had come. Christina had to go to the doctor. Nine months flew by, and she reached out to me to inform me that the doctor was to induce her the following day. I talked it over with my new girlfriend, and she agreed I should be there.

After what I had done to her and not picking up the phone to at least check on her for almost the whole pregnancy, Christina said I should still be there.

Shame, guilt, and remorse became quite frequent visitors in my life, and I could never really shake them unless I was doped up.

The following day I picked her up. As I pulled up to Christina's house, before I could go and knock on the door, she came literally waddling out of the door. She was huge regarding a woman being pregnant. Her scarf was carefully placed around her neck, her coat left open because she couldn't zip it due to our child in her belly. She grabbed the railing and slowly took a step. As she reached the bottom, her eyes squinted which almost looked like she was in pain.

I was so shocked by her appearance, not in a bad way, which I stared like she was some sort of attraction. I hurried and opened my truck door. I ran to her. My humanity side started to kick in.

She grabbed my hand then she wrapped her arms around me the best that she could. "I have missed you so much," she said with a quiver.

I felt horrible, I felt like crawling into a dark corner, AGAIN, to wither away.

"Uhh… I have missed you too," I said as I barricaded any tears from leaving my eyes, "here let me get you to the truck."

Everything was slow motion. I thought about everything that I had done to her, hell to everyone. I thought about my grandma and all of the kind things she did for me to teach me life the best way that she could.

We sat in the driveway for about thirty minutes just talking. I felt like I was supposed to be there with her.

I was meant to be there with her; she was carrying our child. I almost started telling her how horribly sorry I was.

As I was fighting the tears and she was embracing hers, tucked away in my shirt's pocket were some Vicodin. I was trying to do my best not to take any unless I had to. I had finally gotten to the point where I would start to get sick to my stomach, my joints would hurt, and diarrhea would be constant if I did not take them for an extended amount of time. It was almost like hunger. If I didn't eat, I would surely die from starvation, and that is what it felt like going through withdrawals – a slow and painful death.

Addiction itself is a slow painful death like being stabbed to death by many different knives. You poke and prod yourself with so many elements of life that are hard to handle sober, and as your brain busily races trying to make these adjustments, the negative effects of your actions begin to flood your whole conscious.

Before we left her driveway, she did something I did not expect. "Hurry, feel my stomach the baby is moving!" she said with excitement all over her face.

I wasn't sure what to do. I sat there and stared at her stomach before she grabbed my hand placing it on her round and full-of-life belly.

"Oh my god," I said as I tried pulling my hand back, "this is so strange."

She looked at me and smiled as I kept my hand on her stomach for a few more seconds feeling our baby kick my heart into a different direction.

A blissful feeling overcame my whole body. I felt like I was right where I was supposed to be.

When we pulled up to the hospital, a sense of withdrawing came kicking the crap out of bliss, taking over my whole body. Sweat started forming on my forehead. Christina asked if I was okay, I simply told her I was just nervous.

When we finally got her checked into her room, it wasn't long after that a few members of her family showed. Her cousin was going to be in the room while she delivered our child too. She asked him to videotape the whole thing for her. I took the opportunity and ran to the bathroom to take two of the pills I had.

When I returned, one nurse was explaining the induction process, and another was getting all of the medical gear connected to her. It was all so surreal. I couldn't help but think what our child would look like. The nurses said it would be a while before the Pitocin would take effect so I had time to go home and get a change of clothes for the next day. By the sound of it, it would be a few hours before she would deliver.

When I pulled up to my current girlfriend's house, she was outside smoking a cigarette with tears in her eyes. I was concerned that she was upset but not overly worried. Before I left to go back to the hospital, we talked about the situation. She didn't want to be together anymore. I stood there looking at her, not really sure what to say. I somehow always found myself in the most uncomfortable predicaments.

I was kind of mad that she would tell me she wanted to break up when my child was about to be born, but I didn't have time to patch things up. I wanted to hurry back to the hospital, so I didn't miss any more than I already had. I told her fine, and I will get my clothes and anything else later that week. As I drove away, she looked absolutely crushed. I wasn't sure what to do with her, but it only felt right to be part of my child's arrival.

I hurried back to the hospital and when I arrived, still no baby. Christina's cousin was standing in the room, camera in hand, as we awkwardly talked. I knew that a lot of her family did not feel I should be there on the account that I had avoided any responsibility during those previous months. They had every right to be concerned. They were only trying to protect someone they loved.

The doctor made his way to see us and decided he would break her water. Oh, my God... I couldn't believe what he was doing. A flood of liquid rushed from her body forcing our child to move things along.

"Doc, so is it time to deliver?" I asked as my eyes bulged from shock.

The doctor looked at me and smiled. He had a great sense of humor and said, "Nope, we don't get off that easy. I'll be back in probably, I'd say, an hour or so. Maybe a bit longer."

Confused about the whole process I was worried about anything my imagination could conjure up.

Everything was going great until... Christina screamed," Fuck Oh... Shit."

She closed her eyes, her breathing changed, and her soul apparently was overtaken by a demon from the pits of Hell. She was squeezing my hand, so jokingly I blurted, "Oh, come on. It's not that bad."

The demon didn't seem to like my jokes. The demon didn't like them, not one bit.

She turned and looked at me. A flame glared at me from her eyes. "It is not funny! You did this you asshole!" she yelled.

It was about to get serious. Her cousin was coaching her pretty well and for some reason, I was scared for my life. About an hour of contractions getting closer and closer and it was soon time.

My heart started beating like I was doing some extreme cardio workouts. I watched the nurses prop her legs, the doctor suit up, and her cousin press the record button. A feeling came over the room, a feeling of connectedness, a natural feeling that seemed to tune everything else in the world out of my mind. I looked at Christina and admired her for her bravery. I didn't have time for remorse or guilt. I did my best to be as strong as she had been.

She gripped my hand even tighter. The doctor

instructed when to push and when to stop. A woman giving birth is beautifully brutal. I always thought it was push, push, and then baby. The doctor was maneuvering his fingers to help the baby's head out and protect the neck from the umbilical cord.

Christina missed the epidural earlier because of how close her contractions were. When the Anesthesiologist who would give her the epidural said they couldn't we all started to panic. Our baby was coming, and Christina was in indescribable pain. Her screams were horrendous, my hand was very much mush.

"Almost there, give me another big push," the doctor directed.

I could see our child's head. I could see the hair. A pipe must have busted because my eyes were tearing up.

"Ahhh... Shh-Shhh... Oooh... Shh-Shh... Ooh," Christina let out.

"You're doing great Christina, almost there, hold it together," her cousin coached her as he continued to film every minute of life.

"Okay one more big pussshhhh," the doctor directed again.

I stood there holding one of her hands and with my free hand I helped keep her leg in place. I didn't know what to say. Everyone was doing such a great job; I just wanted our child to hurry up and get out of the womb already! I was very anxious to meet our baby.

"One more....," the doctor said. Then, the baby was out. After the head, the baby's body slid right out with ease.

My mouth was wide open, and Christina's breathing returned to normal. The medical staff started using the nose sucker thingy in our child's mouth. Then one of the most beautiful sounds I have ever heard happened.

"Wwwwaaahhhh.... wwwwaaahhhh... Wwwwaaahhh!" our daughter screamed.

I suddenly gasped for air, trying to fight the tears. Our daughter was here. She was so beautiful and perfect. Christina and I looked at one another, smiled, and we kissed.

The doctor asked me if I wanted to cut the cord and I agreed. I couldn't help all the feelings I had and the thoughts of all my past mistakes. I cut the cord in one swipe. Then the doctor drained some blood from the remaining cord. After he was done, the placenta was next. This is an autobiography, not a horror movie so I will save those details.

They allowed both of us to hold her before they started washing the vernix caseosa from her skin. When I held my loosely swaddled daughter for the first time, she was calm, beautiful, and through all of the mess, I created, her eyes were nonjudgmental. She squinted as her hands kept moving around.

Christina was exhausted, my face had traces of stale tears, and her family rejoiced. It was late, so we all called it a night as the nurses took our baby girl and monitored her for the evening so Christina could rest. They gave her some pain medication, and I rushed to the bathroom to give myself my last two pain pills.

I felt withdraws approaching; I wanted this experience to be pain-free. I wish I could say that for the next coming months. The love for my first born daughter just wasn't enough.

Chapter 8
I'll Stop Tomorrow

I couldn't believe that I was a father. Holding my child that I helped create offered some type of magical boost to my humanity level. It was kind of like playing a video game when you find a power-up for your character to be the best you can be and get through obstacles easier, except my obstacle was life. My daughter was my power up temporarily. She allowed me to feel a spark deep inside my soul to do better, to laugh better, to be kinder more often and re-evaluate my life completely.

I decided to cut back on my drinking, and I did. I also decided to cut back on taking all of the pills, but not entirely. I was still taking them almost every day. I had to because avoiding the withdrawals was my number one goal each day.

I didn't move back in with Christina, but I was going over there every day and staying until the evening. I would get up early in the morning and show up at 5:00 a.m. to come help with our daughter and see Christina before I had to be at work.

My daughter was so little, yet so precious. I would hold her in my arms as I fed her a bottle. I always think it is funny when babies make the noises they do when they eat. The faint whimpers, the sucking sound of the bottle, and the irritation they get when they want more. Burping her always scared me. I thought I was going to hurt her so I would tap lightly on her back as I could feel her breath on my neck. Every time that I would feed her and felt her breaths as I burped her, I told myself, "You have to get straight. You have to give her a good life."

About two months of coming and going, Christina and I were getting along, laughing and joking with one another, but she wanted me to stop taking the pills altogether. I would tell her tomorrow I will or when I ran out. It started to feel like she was nagging and trying to control me again.

Coincidentally, ex-girlfriend # 4 was calling me every day. The ex that broke it off the day our daughter was born. She would meet me when I left Christina's house in the evening at my house. I was going back and forth between the two of them, I started taking more pills, and Christina decided it was best that I didn't come over anymore.

I was yet again in a situation of my own making. But this time, I was torn in a different way when I couldn't see my daughter every day.

My friends that I worked with at the cell phone store were awesome and got me some baby stuff I would need at my dad's house for my daughter. They got me things like baby clothes, a pack-n-play, and lotion. I had to make the adjustments; my truck wouldn't work if I were to take my daughter places so I visited my buddy at the dealership. We worked it out where I could trade in my truck for… for… this is going to make me cry, for a sedan. He drove it to me at work and brought all of the paperwork. I was now a proud owner of a four-door Nissan Altima.

With this car, I was able to put my daughter safely in the back, and pick her up and drop her off with her mother.

I was up to about six Vicodin pills a day. Girlfriend # 4 and I were both taking pills so the cost was getting expensive. At the cell phone store, I was pretty bitter when they gave a manager's position to a friend I got a job there; he was there three years less than me. Between the pills, Christina nearly kicking me out of her house, and my employer giving a job to someone that I thought should be mine, it was time to make a change.

I started buying three prescriptions of Vicodin pills from two different people. One guy was somehow getting two scripts per month - one with ninety pills and the other with sixty pills. I was also buying a script from a lady that got sixty every two weeks.

I started lying to girlfriend # 4 about how many I was buying, and I would hide them in an old car radio box in the trunk of my Altima. I was now taking up to fifteen pills a day just to get by. I was spending almost a grand a month on pills. I had to figure something out because my bills were suffering and I was not helping with my daughter.

I slowly stopped seeing my daughter; I had to. The pills became a priority, and the relationship I was in wasn't working. I found someone that had a prescription for Percocet. I had a pretty keen eye for business and hated dabbling with someone selling a few pills here and there, so I always tried to find a bulk supplier. The individual sold me two scripts a month. Every two weeks they got sixty pills, and this would cost me about six hundred dollars a month. I was still buying the guy's script of Vicodin of ninety a month.

I was taking four or five Percocet a day, sometimes more, and I would always run out before the guy could get his next script filled. So I had the Vicodin to hold me over, but I had to start taking three to four at a time just to maintain myself because I became used to the potency of the Percocet. My life was spiraling quickly out of control. Every night when I would go to bed, I would look at girlfriend # 4. I hated the position that I was in, always telling myself I would quit tomorrow, and I will patch things up with Christina and get my family back.

This talk went on for a while until one day at work a gentleman walked through the front doors. He had semi-long white hair that stopped at his neck, a thick white goatee, and a black leather vest with patches covering it accompanied by black pants and black leather shoes.

The guy I was working with whispered to me that this guy was in a "motorcycle club." When he turned around so we could see the back of his vest, we saw the "club's" name. For my safety, the "club" will remain nameless.

He was loud, and his presence made us feel uncomfortable. When he made his way to the counter, we read a diamond shaped patch that said 1%-ers (one-percenters). Rumor has it what that patch means so I treated him as nicely as possible that day. The patch didn't refer to the one percent of billionaires represented in the United States. My sense of humor kicked in because I knew everyone loved a good laugh.

He wanted a leather case to protect his cell phone. So I made a joke and said, "Hey, I tell you what. I will give you the case for free, and maybe if I run into some trouble you could offer a one-time protection deal or take care of my problem."

He looked at me, my coworker, and started laughing. He didn't say anything, just laughed. He began to reach for something out of his back pocket, and I cannot lie, all of a sudden I got really nervous. My coworker and I looked at one another as our eyes got as big as baseballs. Then... he pulled out his wallet.

"I'll take the case, and I do appreciate it," he said as he pulled out a business card, "take this card and come down to the clubhouse house sometime. I'll get you a few drinks and a few ladies. If anyone gives you any trouble, I'll take care of 'em. When you come just tell them, I sent ya."

I grabbed the card and read it before I put it in my wallet. It had his cell number and the clubhouse information on it. For whatever distorted reason, even though the stereotype of bikers flooded my mind, I was intrigued to have that card and fantasized if I ever needed "backup" what he could do. I would not run into him until months later.

I was going through withdrawals on a bi-weekly basis. I would always run out of pills, and it was getting harder to keep my drug use a secret. Everyone at first thought I was just sick all of the time because that is how

I played it off, but I am pretty sure some had me pegged for the truth.

I decided to leave my job at the cell phone store. I still had a significant resentment that my friend was a manager at one of our other locations. I started working with the guy that first introduced me to buying Vicodin on the street. He was taking pills, I was taking pills, and when I started at the lawn fertilization company, almost every single one of us on the sales staff were taking pills.

At this job, I was working more hours and made a little bit more money. That extra money didn't help me get ahead, like I wanted, or help my daughter. We would get an hour lunch break and take our pills and go shopping or drive around St. Clair County. If I wasn't the one driving, I couldn't help but stare out the window and ponder my meaning, my existence, and my purpose. The effects of the drugs were starting to lose their power on my reality. I began thinking about life, and as a result, I was becoming saddened, even when I used. I couldn't shake it until the Oxycontin found me.

I was still going to bed at night wanting to quit. It is kind of like wanting to lose weight and longing to get healthier; we tell ourselves we will go to the gym tomorrow. Then tomorrow becomes today and then today becomes yesterday. When it is all said and done, our initial goal to our personal betterment becomes nothing but a failed memory making many of us state what we think is obvious, a what-is-the-point attitude.

A forty milligram oxycontin found me one night when I was with girlfriend # 4, my friend who got me the job at the lawn fertilization company, and his girlfriend. He cleaned off the yellowish coating and took the end of his lighter to crush it up on his counter. I had never snorted anything in my life, but within a few minutes that was about to change. He took his driver's license to break the little white pieces up into finer pieces. All of them knew I had never snorted anything. The three of them knew I was hesitant, but they insisted that I try the oxycontin. I really didn't want to. I knew how much I loved the Percocet and Vicodin. They kept pressuring me, saying things like, "You will like it better than the other pills," and "It is only a small line, you won't even get that high." Everything inside me told me to leave, just go. I left the kitchen pissed off and stormed out of the front door so I could get some air. As I stood in his front yard, I looked up to the moon. I started to think about my daughter and Christina. I am not sure if demons are real but at that exact moment, it felt like the whispers from a mouth of the damned slowly breathed doubt into me that night. I kept thinking to myself, "Don't do it, Ty. Just go. Your Grandma Bechel always told you to just leave if you found yourself in an unwanted situation and call someone who cares." The demon breath chilled my bones as I started talking myself into doing the oxycontin and disregarding my grandmother's warning. I didn't have anyone to call that would care, I thought. I finally felt like a failure.

My moment of inner conflict was broken when the front door opened. I looked over my shoulder, and it was girlfriend # 4. She walked over to me and put both of her arms on each one of my shoulders. She looked me in the eyes and said that it is only a little bit and that I would enjoy it. I turned my back on the moon's comforting light and gave in to the whispers of madness.

It was my turn. The small little white line was still resting comfortably on the counter. I held the pen tubing in my hand. I thought to myself whether I should really be doing this but that thought fleeted very quickly as I looked at all three of them staring at me like I was some sort of carnival attraction. I liked the Vicodin and Percocet too much. Everyone that I knew that had done oxycontin only had good things to say about the feeling, especially these guys. I sat there for thirty seconds or so, contemplating… "What the hell," I thought to myself. Up my nose the powder went. Within a minute I was already feeling the effects. My head was lighter than it has ever felt and my pain and worries were gone forever - at least until the oxycontin wore off. Under the influence of Oxycontin, I was able to talk to customers on the phone better, sell better, and forget my daughter better.

From that moment forward, after I had taken my first dose of what I thought was artificial heaven, I was never the same until I would decide to make the most crucial decision in my adult life. The pain I was about to cause everyone was beyond anything my family and I could have ever imagined. If Clarence could have only visited and shown me how I would end up if I kept going like he did with George, I would have surely stopped "tomorrow."

Chapter 9
Bombs Away

Girlfriend # 4 started working with me at the lawn fertilization company. She worked the front office; I worked the sales room. Together we were making enough money to barely support both of our drug habits. She preferred smoking weed and taking Xanax, but she would never pass up a chance to do some oxycontin.

One day on our hour lunch break, two days before payday, she and I went to lunch together, alone. I ran out of money and all of my pills the previous evening. We only had enough cash from my change that was in my car for something from the dollar menu at one of the fast-food chains. I was starting to go through the beginning stage of withdrawals by this time. You could always feel the withdrawals creeping up on you. It was almost as if the withdrawals were stalking you – in a way they were. You would always look over your shoulder hoping no one was there, but the paranoia that something or someone was chasing you was inevitable. Then like a ninja in the night, they attack. Your full blown flu-like-symptoms-times-fifty hits you full circle. Luckily for me, when we were sitting in the parking lot of the fast-food joint she pulled out a small, personal sized Altoids tin container.

I looked at her with confusion. I wasn't sure if she was saying I had bad breath or that because we didn't have any money and an Altoid was our dessert.

"Open it, I got you something," she eagerly said.

My forehead was starting to sweat and I was not thrilled about opening a gift in an Altoid tin can. But to appease her, I opened it. I looked and had to readjust my eyes to make sure what I was seeing was real. I smiled ear to ear in astonishment that she would get me something so great. My panic of the painful withdrawals quickly subsided. She had gotten us four eighty milligram oxycontin tabs.

"Oh my God, you are the best," I said as I continued to smile.

"Hurry, crush one of those up," she urgently demanded.

My heart was racing with excitement knowing that I wouldn't have to battle the sickness while I was at work.

It hit me like a ton of bricks as I was crushing the pill. This was like some sick, twisted version of the story The Gift of the Magi. My happiness started to get punched in the face by my usually silenced conscious. "What are you doing? This is how your life is going to be?" I thought to myself as my conscious was doing its best to grab my attention.

"Wait a sec. How'd you get these? We're broke," I asked with the powder divided up evenly on the CD case.

She smiled at me, "Well, I got three of them fronted and took sixty dollars I had saved and bought one."

If any of you are wondering, an eighty mil Oxy would go for anywhere from forty to sixty dollars. And when you are addicted and about to go through the pain of withdrawals, you will pay that.

"Hmm…" I muttered.

I knew this wasn't the life I wanted. It seemed like every time I would start to talk myself into something positive and better, those whispers of madness would come back.

"Just do it. The withdrawals are sitting right over there waiting. You don't do it then they will devour you." Invariably, these were the thoughts I would get.

So to shut up the voices, I snorted my share, passing the CD case and tooter to her. Within a minute the sweat stopped, the dull knee pain quit, and a smile was permanent for the rest of the day. We didn't even bother ordering any food, we didn't have to. Our appetite was fed with what it exactly wanted and needed – dopamine.

We made it to payday so on lunch she and I went to cash our check. We sped to the guy she got the Oxycontin from and paid our fronted bill. Come to find out we had to pay eighty dollars apiece for the fronted pills before he would sell us anymore. I didn't care; I took my last pill that morning. I paid the two-hundred and forty dollars plus bought a handful more. Between her and me, we didn't have much money left. I had to have enough to pay my car payment, which I did directly after leaving the dealer's house. I knew if I didn't I would spend the rest of the money on pills. She had one hundred dollars left, and I only had twenty dollars left. I had enough money to get food from the dollar menu somewhere for a few days. It was always a dollar sandwich and water, just enough food not to starve.

You get to the point where you don't eat to be healthy or gain energy. You literally eat because you know if you do not you would get sick and wouldn't be able to do drugs anymore. Food becomes only necessary as a supplement to get you through until your next high. By this point, the drugs have taken the royal seat and have become your master. You start doing as it says, never questioning it because the repercussions were always negative and severe. Withdrawals were the executioner.

We had enough pills to get us through to the following Friday; we only made it to Wednesday, five days later. I began rationing my pill inventory, but I wasn't very good at it. I would split the eighty-milligram oxy into fourths and do one line when my buzz would start to wear off. I always did more than I planned.

Thursday came, girlfriend # 4 didn't even bother to show up to work, and I called off saying I was sick. By Friday, one day later, my boss called me explaining that they didn't need me any longer. Girlfriend # 4 also said she had to get her life straight so we broke up, again.

Friday I was at my dad's to suffer through the withdrawals. I was bouncing back and forth from his house, and girlfriend # 4's so my bedroom was still

71

available to me as I entered my dark room - depressed, alone, and scared how bad I was about to start hurting. Before I laid down for the next few uncomfortable days, I went and got two big glasses of water, a few saltine crackers, and sat them on my nightstand along with my cigarettes and lighter. I went and took a quick five-minute shower because I knew that I probably wouldn't be taking a shower for at least two days.

After I had been done with the shower, I did manage to tell my dad that I was not feeling well. I am pretty sure he knew what was going on, but I played it off like I was coming down with a virus. I walked into my bedroom and turned the television on but kept the volume very low. I made sure the curtains wouldn't let any bright light in, and I shut and locked the door. Bright lights and semi-loud noises would bother my eyes and hurt my ears. I became very sensitive when my body was doing its best to expel the poison I put in it every day.

I rested my head on the pillow as I stared at my alarm clock – 2:00 p.m. As each minute passed, I could feel the withdrawals getting more powerful. My stalker suddenly became my attacker. I looked at my alarm clock again – 3:02 p.m. Every part of me was trying to wake up from the constant numbing I had caused with the drugs. Not being use to feeling, the slightest brush against my skin would hurt. The drugs didn't just shut off my feelings they also shut off my body to most basic pain.

Suddenly my stomach started to gurgle, and my mouth tasted like an aftertaste of bad food, which wouldn't leave. I hopped out of bed and ran to the bathroom. I almost didn't make it to the toilet as the fecal matter left my body right before I could sit down on the seat. My nausea now turned into a regurgitation of regret. I had to quickly grab the trash can as I vomited nothing but a yellowish-brown liquid.

I made it back to my room after washing my mouth out the best that I could. I felt I was in some form of vertigo. I tried smoking a cigarette, but it tasted really gross; I was only able to take a few drags – enough to keep the nicotine cravings away.

I was trying my best to fall asleep, and it wasn't working. I couldn't get comfortable in the bed, and I rearranged my pillow I don't know how many times. I kept kicking the blankets around because my legs felt like someone was trying to break out of my flesh from the inside out. My wrists were hurting, even my fingertips. I closed my eyes and dozed off what felt like a few hours. I opened my eyes and stared at the alarm clock – 4:11 p.m. After time was not moving along at all, I turned my clock around so I couldn't keep looking at the painful reminder that I was going through withdrawals.

I was getting very nervous because the second full day of withdrawals was always worse than the first. As sick as this sounds, sometimes to try and make myself feel better I would try and masturbate and get a quick spike in my serotonin, oxytocin, and whatever other natural chemicals get released during the climax to help me feel better even if for a brief moment and assist me in sleep. I would take large amounts of over the counter pain medication like Tylenol or Ibuprofen to numb the pain. Nothing seemed to work.

The second day came, and I laid there crying, begging for the pain to stop. I prayed to whatever was listening to take it all away.

The pain didn't go away but by the fourth day, I was able to finally keep some food down. My joints were not hurting as bad, but I needed to figure something out. I wanted to get some Oxy, but I wouldn't have any money until I got my last paycheck. I sat there and started to brainstorm.

My wallet! I remembered I had a number in there that may be able to help me. I should have just kept going without taking any more pills, but all I could think about was getting high. I was in desperation mode to get high.

You will rack your brain thinking of the last possible way to score a high. I grabbed my wallet out of my pants. I pulled out the business card and held it as I contemplated if I should open that door. I wasn't exactly sure what I should say when I called the biker from the cell phone store. I just knew I probably should play it safe.

I dialed the number, and it started ringing. "This is (blank)," he answered.

I froze for a second, almost convinced to hang up.

"Uh... hey, this is the guy from the cell store," I stuttered.

He started laughing like he did in the store so I started laughing with him.

"Well how are ya little buddy?" he asked.

"I am good, I actually had something I needed to talk to you about but not over the phone. I am looking for something," I instructed him.

"Smart move, yeah just come to where I am at, and we will see if I can help you out."

I had a smile come over my face because being in a biker "club" he would surely know where to get what I was looking for.

"Great I will be there shortly."

I hung up the phone, put on some clothes, and grabbed my keys. I was hoping that he would have something for me, a pill, lead, something. I was going there with no money, but I was banking that he would do a favor for the case I helped him out with.

I made it to the location he gave me, and he was on an industrial type machine. He saw me as he waved me in his direction. He killed the engine as I climbed the ten foot or so ladder to get to him.

I made it to the top as he sat in the driver's seat of this weird machine then he said, "Give me your phone and lift up your shirt."

I have never been checked for what I could only assume was surveillance equipment he was looking for.

"You're clean, so what's up man?" he asked.

Still feeling awkward from my light frisking I replied, "Not much, I came here to see if you can get..." I attempted to say as he interrupted me by starting the loud engine of this machine.

"Okay, just yell into my ear," he said as he pointed to his ear.

I screamed, "I need some Oxycontin, you have any?"

He leaned into my ear, "No, don't really mess with them but I should be able to get you some. Give me a week and I will get back with you."

My face fell flat with disappointment. I leaned back into his ear, "Okay, yeah let me know for sure. Later."

He nodded as I stepped down the ladder. I struck out. I wouldn't have my final paycheck for a few days so I wasn't sure what I could do. So I went back home and was somehow able to convince my dad to get me a few Vicodin from a neighbor's house. It wasn't what I was looking for, but it took the edge off for a little bit.

Three days went by, and I was still bone dry on pills then my phone rang. It was the biker. Without hesitation, I answered it.

"Hey (blank) how are you doing?" I politely asked hoping he had some good news for me.

"Hey partner, I am good. I have what we talked about. I am going to have you meet my girl, and she will give them to you. And you will just pay me later."

Pay later? That was good news, sort of, maybe?

"What if I can't pay?"

He laughed as usual and said, "Oh, you will, some way you will. She is on her way so go to the meeting place, and she will fill you in on the details."

Hesitant to answer I muttered, "Okay, on my way."

"She'll see you soon," he replied.

I didn't know exactly what I was about to get myself into, but something ugly was about to be born.

Chapter 10

An Opiate Orgasm

I met the biker's girlfriend at a discreet location. When I pulled up, she was already waiting. When she stepped out of her car, she didn't look much like a biker's girlfriend. She was around fifty years old, wrinkles slightly invaded her face, and she wore regular clothes. I guess I was expecting a woman dressed in all leather and her head partially shaved in rebellion.

We stood and got acquainted for a few minutes until she handed be the small baggy of eighty-milligram Oxycontin. They were all bunched together like a nest full of eggs almost cuddling one another. I was excited beyond belief because I knew within five minutes I would quit feeling so depressed.

She said I would owe her boyfriend six hundred dollars so to call them when I sold them all. Wait a minute sell all of them? For some reason, I was thinking he was going to give me some for free for the leather case. The street value of the oxycontin at the time was higher than one measly leather case. A case retailed around twenty bucks.

I didn't lose my composure but inside I was panicking. I had never sold anything before. I tried to sell weed once but freaked out when my car smelled like a marijuana nursery and the thought of getting caught deterred me from selling.

"How many are here?" I asked.

She smiled and politely said, "Fifteen. It won't matter what you do with them really as long as you get his money to him no later than two weeks. He is very fond of his pennies."

I looked at her and smiled. I ran the math quickly in my head and determined he was selling them to me for forty dollars apiece, and people are willing to pay sixty dollars. If I do sell them, then I would get five for free.

"Okay, no problem," I said as I looked at my phone to check the time.

Calmly she smiled and walked away, "See ya."

I quickly got in the car, cleaned off the coating, and crushed it up. I was moving fast like we do when we have to pee really badly. I didn't feel that I was moving fast enough. Then I managed to get it together and my mild aches and constant thoughts of being a crappy father left.

I pulled away from the meeting place and started calling a few people that I had used with before. I was able to get a hold of an old buddy so we met up and figured out a way to get rid of the rest and keep the extra for ourselves.

Somehow I managed to land a job at another cell phone store which was a different service provider than where I worked before. I was able to get rid of most of the Oxycontin but kept the extras my using buddy made from getting rid of them. I was able to keep a few extra too because I got my small final paycheck from the lawn fertilization company.

Things were going okay. I started this new job and was doing pretty well as long as I had my drugs. There were days I would run out and couldn't find anything before work. I would be sick waiting on customers. There was a cell phone costume the store would use for marketing purposes. It was a costume you would wear and stand at a road and wave like a fool. I would sleep on the costume and ask some of the employees to wake me only if they needed me. I would only do this if the managers were not there.

I was having trouble paying for my car because, even though I started getting free oxy's, I shortly quit getting them free. I started spending most of my paycheck to buy them myself. The buddy I had help me with the oxy would split the cost with me every once in a while. Other than that, I was like a selfish child with their toys. Mine!

Miraculously, I was able to find another connection of forty milligram Oxycontin. The guy I was getting these from supposedly survived pancreatic cancer so he personally sold me his whole script. I was able to get them very cheap, and this opened another door like it did in high school with all the liquor I could get at the liquor store.

At work, I managed to keep my composure and remembered to eat more often. I didn't want people to think that I was a junkie, but I knew I was becoming one.

I owed the biker about three hundred dollars, and I avoided him because I didn't have it. I was doing my best to keep up with the other guy I was getting them from and sometimes I would buy Vicodin to lessen the withdrawals.

Then one day my using buddy and I were at my grandpa's. We would find ourselves there from time to time, and my grandfather didn't seem to mind. We were in the basement, and he would talk about shooting oxy. He would go into detail of how great it felt and how the rush was unbelievable. I told him I would never do that, but that held no weight a few minutes later.

He pulled out an unopened bag of hypodermic needles. I looked at him with one of those "what are you doing" looks.

"Go get a spoon," he said as he was taking the filter out of a new cigarette.

"I don't know man. I like snorting them, like a lot," I reluctantly said.

As standoffish as I was, I went upstairs and grabbed a spoon.

When I made it back downstairs, he ripped the bag of needles opened and handed me one. He pulled out his own spoon then gave me a cap full of water.

"Just watch, it is pretty easy," he said.

I watched him with an uneasy feeling mixed with excitement. I was curious about how it felt.

It was almost ritualistic how he did everything so precisely from the prepping of his instrument to giving himself the dose.

His eyes fluttered, and his face was all smiles. He looked at me, "One sec man, I will help you."

I smiled back and started breaking up my pill. He did the rest from there, grabbed my needle, and directed me to give him my hand.

I took a deep breath through my nose, gave him my left hand, and cringed at what he was about to do. I wasn't much of a fan of needles. I felt the piercing of my skin and oddly enough I could hear the faint pop when he broke my skin. It felt like it was taking forever then…

A fiery presence quickly traveled up my arm. My head and chest seemed as if they fell to the ground as I closed my eyes and let out, "Woah!" It was a feeling, which could possibly be debated to be better than sex.

That was it, I swore I would never do Oxycontin, and I swore I would never do oxy intravenously. My buddy and I sat there and chatted for a bit. When the high started to wear off, I had a sudden feeling of doom and regret.

I was using three to five times a day and would shoot the oxy every once in a while. As much as I loved the feeling, I didn't want people to see the marks.

I was talking to Christina again, but I was so out of it most of the time; I still think to this day she cared for me so much that she felt sorry for me and the direction I was heading. My bills were suffering - what was left that I was paying - and I was about to lose my car so I convinced her to pay for my car payment, and let me tell you that it was more than four hundred dollars a month. I actually cared about her, but I cared more about the drugs. Deep down, I think she had a hope that she could save me.

I was not spending a dime to help Christina and my daughter, but I was begging her to help me salvage my car – not once but twice. Two months, she paid for my car I voluntarily had repossessed anyways. Before I turned over my car, I asked my aunt, my dad's sister, to borrow a thousand dollars to buy a used 1993 Nissan Sentra. My aunt helped me with no questions asked.

I was still unable to see how sick I was becoming, and I reached out to a friend that sold me my Nissan Altima. He was able to get me a job selling cars. I did my best to cut back my drug use, so I only did oxy here and there but continued to use Vic's, and perc's whenever I would get my hands on them.

I started working at the dealership, and I was downright horrible at selling cars. I was a wreck, a mess, a complete and utter tragedy. I was always questioning myself every day – confidence found the first jet outta town. I could memorize the specs of the new cars but was having a tough time speaking to customers. After about two weeks of being employed, I discovered almost everyone at the dealership was taking pills like Vicodin, even ecstasy.

I got some oxy one night after work and went to meet my sister at a party. Everyone was drinking and doing cocaine. I was there for about five minutes, and someone asked if I wanted some "the white stuff." I didn't hesitate to try some. I was already high on oxy, and did two shots of whiskey to catch up with the rest of the drinkers, and then a powdery line was placed before me. I sucked it up through the straw into my nose. From the combination of oxy and liquor, I was lighter on my feet than Muhammad Ali. Then, within a minute of doing the cocaine, I ran to the trash can and threw up. A couple of people told me that sometimes happens the first time you do it. From that moment forward, I started mixing oxy and cocaine together whenever I had the chance.

I was only employed at the dealership for about two more weeks after the weekend of doing cocaine. I managed to blame my situation on the job and everyone else. I decided to reach out to the owners of the first cell phone store I worked at.

They said I could come back and that it was great timing that I had contacted them. They needed a manager for one of their locations. It would include a high hourly wage plus commission and a monthly store bonus. Don't ask me how I pulled this off because, like I stated a few paragraphs earlier, I was completely a mess.

I came back and ran a small cell phone shop. I was fully reconnected with the biker. I found out that he was doing cocaine all of the time, and we started having late night cocaine and oxycontin binges. Some people call this a "speedball." One night, in particular, we did eight eighty milligram Oxycontin and an eight-ball of cocaine together. I started to spiral even quicker. The 1993 Nissan Sentra I bought broke down, so I had my brother and his friend try to fix it. They broke it even more. So I managed to get it to my dad's house, where I was staying at the time, and parked it.

My sister had a 1990's Ford Taurus that her grandmother allowed me to make payments on so I could keep going to work. I was burning through my paychecks very quickly. From buying cocaine and Oxycontin, I would spend some of my days in my office, with the door closed, on the floor in agony. I would ask the employees working to watch the store and come get me only if necessary. I was now a full blown junkie, and I knew it.

I would have the biker's girlfriend meet me at work and front me oxy whenever her biker boyfriend wouldn't know. He eventually found out, yelling at me, threatening me to never do business without him knowing.

He said just pay him, and nothing would happen to me. Between his cocaine problem and my oxy/cocaine problem, paranoia set in.

He invited me to his house one night. As I walked through the front door, he wasn't sitting in the kitchen as he normally was when I would arrive. I heard some faint moaning coming from the back.

"Hello?" I yelled from the kitchen as I stood there with a good idea of what I was hearing.

I heard whispers, then, "Hey, come back here," the biker said, "we are in the bedroom."

I slowly walked through the hallway, hoping to give them enough time to dress, if, in fact, that is what they were doing. I stepped through the bedroom door and... the biker was on his side, directly behind his girlfriend, as they were both completely naked.

Embarrassed, I turned around, "Sorry, I'll come back."

The biker said between his moans, "Nonsense, get in here. The table there, that's your line of oxy and coke."

I looked at the drug mixture staring at me and suddenly didn't care that the two of them were having sex. As I grabbed the tooter and began to fix the aches I was feeling, I heard the noises of their affairs happening directly behind me.

"Come on baby, yeah," the biker said as the bed squeaked.

Her moans, of what I assumed were pleasure, made me even more uncomfortable. I finished doing the line then they both said together, "Come here, drop your drawers."

My eyes widened, and my anxiety flew through the roof. Stuttering, I could only reply with, "Nah. That's okay. I... um... I am okay, just holler at me when you're done," as I tried to leave the bedroom.

"You better get your fucking ass over here and finish her off. She wants you, so make it happen," the biker demanded.

I watched him penetrate her from behind, and I just wanted to leave. I was scared too. He had a very nasty temper when he didn't get what he wanted.

"Nah, I don't want too," I sheepishly muttered.

His look of content switched to anger as he started

to get off of the bed.

"Okay, fine, I'll drop my pants," I said to prevent him from getting any closer to me.

His girlfriend tried to seduce me and get me involved. I was too nervous and with the copious amounts of drugs, my blood flow was only working enough to keep me alive. Finally, they both said forget it that we will try again later. I pulled up my pants, and we never tried again later, we just did a large amount of cocaine and oxy – thankfully.

The biker must have owed someone money for cocaine or something because he asked me to find him some a few weeks after the bedroom incident. I didn't have any connections except for my sister and him. So I got his money and met my sister to get him the cocaine.

I met my sister, and we got ripped off. I had over two hundred dollars of this biker's money invested in drugs and nothing to show for it. His girlfriend was waiting for us, so, fortunately, he was not there. I told her I would get the money and be in touch the next day.

The only thing I could think of because I was broke, was to not do an IOU at work and pay the money back when I could. That would buy me some time until I got paid.

Soon after the cocaine debacle, after I paid back the IOU, a friend wanted to borrow my car to go to St. Louis and get some buttons. I was unfamiliar with what that was at the time, and they told me it was heroin. They offered me some money and a few buttons in trade. They dropped me off at work and picked me back up a few hours later. I told the employee I was working with that day that I needed to leave early to drop off the deposit at the bank. I hadn't made a deposit in almost two weeks.

After we had driven away from my work, we pulled into a parking lot so I could try the heroin. I was pretty doped up already from doing oxycontin that morning so I wasn't too scared or thrilled to do the dope. They poured me some out on a CD case, and I snorted it. I didn't feel much on account of the Oxy, I guess, or it was a weak mixture.

I was going to stop by the bank but decided I would drop them off and stop by a branch by my house. By this time, I was living back at my mom's. My dad and I had a falling out which was due to my drug use. They gave me some money and two caps for my trouble.

The following morning I woke up and decided to give my buddy a call to tell him I had two buttons. He said he would be right over after he stopped by the drug store to pick up the needles.

I was nervous. Now that I wasn't completely high out of my mind, I wasn't sure if I should do heroin like that. I had seen the movie "Trainspotting," and the withdrawals were supposedly worse than oxy. I wanted nothing to do with them either.

He made it to my house in about fifteen minutes. Christina and I were not talking, and I hadn't seen my daughter in a long time. I said what the hell. My mom was at work, and nothing was there to bother us, except the dogs. And I am pretty sure they weren't telling anybody.

He came in, and I grabbed two spoons from the kitchen and a cigarette from my pack to pull out the filter. We did the usual routine, and I handed him my needle. I gave him my hand then he pushed the plunger in. Just like the first time I shot oxy, a fiery feeling rushed up my arm.

I would say not even ten seconds went by, and every inch of my body was forgiven of any past harm that I had done to it. The other drugs were just stages that were prepping me for my moment I would transcend to heaven on Earth. The enlightenment phases were complete; the Four Noble Truths were finally understood that day as I had finally found Nirvana. I no longer needed a woman's touch, a friend's laughter, a mother's understanding, and I definitely didn't need help with anything, from anybody. I could finally fly. If I would have only known that the wings were temporary and artificial. An opiate orgasm was released that day. I would spend the next coming months chasing it to the ends of the Earth.

Chapter 11

Every Great Empire Has Fallen

After doing the heroin, my buddy and I went our separate ways for the day. I did some cleaning around the house, and was trying to find something to do for the evening. I still didn't go to the bank and deposit the money.

Someone I knew called and said he and his friend needed a ride somewhere. I went and picked them up. I kept the deposit with me, because I was scared someone would take it. When I picked them up, there was three of them and they had been drinking. For whatever reason one of the passengers needed change for a one hundred dollar bill so I made it.

I dropped them off and stopped to get something to eat. I wanted to get some cocaine to mix with the remaining oxy I had. Ever since their proposition, I was trying to avoid the biker and his girlfriend unless I had to get oxy's from them.

The evening came, so I went to a bar. I was surely able to find some cocaine. Downtown Wood River bars always had it floating around somewhere. I walked into the bar and started asking around. Someone I knew bought me a few drinks as I continued my search. I ran to the bathroom and snorted a half of an eighty milligram oxy. When I was in the bathroom conducting a meeting with my "boss," I found some cocaine.

I started drinking more heavily, and the night started to get blurry. Last thing I remembered was being on the dance floor with a girl I didn't know.

I woke up on my mom's couch, in a panic. I couldn't remember anything about the night as I sat straight up. The deposit! I hurried and ran out to my car to check under the seat where I remembered having it last. I saw the bag and I was relieved until I looked it in to count the money.

In my foggy haze after a night of liquor, oxy, and cocaine, I suddenly felt like vomiting. Not from the hangover effects but from the bank bag that wasn't holding any money. All that was left was checks and a deposit slip.

I started crying. Everything was going to start to make sense to everyone. My drug use was going to start being questioned and why I am sick all of the time. I was terrified. I couldn't remember if I spent the money which would have been a lot – about fourteen hundred dollars. I had to be at work on Monday, the following day. I started thinking of jail and wherever else my imagination took me.

I had never been arrested and didn't even have something as simple as a speeding ticket. Through my stupor, I called a friend I knew in Arizona. He struggled with drugs and I wanted to get away so I could clean up. We talked for about an hour. He gave me his address and said I could stay with him so I could attempt to get clean.

I was very hesitant. Monday came, and I was a no-show. The owner's son from the cell phone store was calling, and we talked a little bit. He knew I was doing drugs because we did them together.

As we sat on the phone, I kept thinking how am I going to explain any of this to them. They were great to me and I took their trust and threw it in the trash like everyone else I came into contact with.

"Hey, pops wants to talk at ya, so don't go running. It will only make things worse," the owner's son said.

I sat there for what felt like an hour breathing on the phone, ready to break down even more crying in regret and fear.

"I'll be there," I told him.

I didn't go. My mom kept asking what was wrong because I started packing my trunk full of clothes, printed out driving directions to Arizona, and told my mom bye. I didn't tell her or anyone where I was going.

I got in my car and drove. Before I left town, I cashed my last paycheck from the cell store, I grabbed a couple of Vicodin and pot for my withdrawals. I gassed up the Ford Taurus and started driving. I drove, and drove, and drove. Four hours or so went by, and I started having withdrawals.

I am not sure what town I was in but I pulled up and there was a gas station, a motel, and a restaurant next to one another. I went and paid for a room and asked where exactly I was because I had been driving for a while. I do not remember the name of the city but they told me I was only forty-five minutes from Branson, MO.

I checked myself into the motel and started to smoke the weed to help with the pain. I took the Vic's I had a few hours later which didn't do much for the withdrawals.

I felt stoned but hurt like hell. It was an awkward feeling. I paid for four days at the motel. The first two days, I denied any housekeeping services.

As I laid on the paper thin comforter at this third rate motel, I couldn't quit vomiting. As usual, even the insides of my ears hurt.

There was a small television, which sat directly towards the end of the bed on top of the dresser. I let it play on one channel. It was stuck on Encore. They were having their free special to encourage people to sign up for their service, I guess.

Between the picture going in and out, the same movies kept playing over and over. It was Shanghai Knights with Owen Wilson and Jackie Chan, The One with Jet Li, and Coyote Ugly with Piper Perabo.

People kept calling me, including the biker, the owner's son, and my mom. I texted my mom and said I would be okay and that I had to detox myself. She had heard what was going on.

The biker kept calling and leaving voicemails. If I went too long without talking to him, his temper definitely showed.

I listened to a handful of messages from him and each one got angrier and meaner. Towards the last one he threatened me if I didn't call him back.

Three days had gone by and I finally got enough courage to take a shower and shave. I was feeling a little better, not much, so I went to the diner and ordered some food. As I sat there at the table I could have swore people were staring at me. I was almost certain that they could tell I wasn't from around there so I asked my waitress to make my order to go.

After nearly three days of not eating, the food tasted pretty good. I had biscuits and gravy, with two over-easy eggs, and a slab of ham steak. I was feeling much better after eating but I was still craving drugs, badly.

Day four came, and I packed up my stuff and decided to go home. I knew going to Arizona was only prolonging my situation. When I got on Highway 255 in Missouri, I called the biker. He was actually nice and asked what was going on.

I asked him if he happened to have anything, and as usual he did. Even though I was feeling better, I sped to his place.

I went on a weeklong bender before confessing everything to my mom. I needed help. She called Christina and we all began calling places.

Finally, I was able to go to a detox/rehab center in Quincy, Illinois. My mom and Christina dropped me off, and directly after detox, I was supposed to start a twenty-eight day treatment program.

I made it a day and a half. It was miserable and my withdrawals were already back, full swing. I thought the staff was rude plus I was probably a little difficult to deal with. The rooms were cold and the "television" room might as well been a padded cell because that is what it felt like.

I called mom and Christina; they refused to come

and get me. The staff member that was working called a few people for me, even the biker. They told her if I made it to a location where they could wire money they would transfer some so I could get home until we found out how much it would cost.

I wanted to leave. I wanted out of there that minute. They told me since I decided to leave that I couldn't stay there and wait. So I packed my green duffle bag full of clothes and started walking down the main strip in Quincy.

I wasn't sure what I was going to do. I had no money and only a calling card with about twenty minutes worth of calls on it.

In the distance I could see a Super 8. I could go there and use a lobby phone or something.

I walked through the lobby doors and immediately told the receptionist that my car broke down and that I needed to contact someone. She was very nice.

I called the guy I shot the heroin with the first time. He said no. I called and begged mom and Christina and they said no. Finally, I called a girl that liked me when I was working at the second cell phone store and she agreed to get me.

She got there relatively fast. She was trying to ask what I was doing in Quincy, so I gave her some lame excuse. I didn't dare tell her it was because of drugs.

I had her drive me to the biker's house so I could get a fix. The withdrawals were in the beginning stages of their brutality, so I told her a friend was in from town and I wanted to stop and say hi.

She sat in the car for nearly an hour until I came out high on oxy, cocaine, and two Xanax pills. She drove me to my mom's, and I went inside. I don't even think I said thank you, needless to say, this was the last time we ever spoke.

My mom was not happy and Christina refused to talk to me. The following day, my mom said I needed to get a job. I didn't know where to turn. I tried to get another sales job, but I was a wreck. I finally reached out the second pancake joint I worked at in high school.

I was miserable. I was going backwards. I went from making forty thousand dollars a year to a measly minimum wage job.

I was taking what I made and only spending it on drugs. The guy I used heroin with for the first time turned me onto a guy in Wood River which very well may have been the cause of many to become addicted to heroin. Nestled behind a car dealership was a group of apartments. In this bungalow of lost souls, I was there with them all.

The guy selling the heroin would have people come over, grab a bag of needles, and insist that they try it that way. Most people then were just snorting but he managed to get them hooked intravenously. I started hanging out over there and getting free heroin here and there for giving them rides.

I was trying to keep the Ford Taurus but all of my money was going to heroin. I wasn't sure what to do because my sister's grandma wanted the car back or a payment. So, I took one hundred and seventy-five dollars from my mom to pay for it so I could keep the car.

I was doing heroin every day and my diet consisted of gummy worms, potato chips, and Mountain Dew. The guy selling the heroin wanted to expand his operations and asked if I would sell some and in turn get some free dope. I took the nugget of raw heroin he was getting from a guy across 367 (The Clark Bridge) and went home. I had a tourniquet hidden at my mom's and I went on a three day binge. I preferred to use by myself for a few reasons and one of them was so I didn't have to share.

On the third day, shortly before my mom got home from work, I did a "blast" of heroin in her bathroom. I remember getting dizzy then I blacked out. I was woken by my mom shaking me. I am not sure if I overdosed or just nodded out and stayed asleep. Some may consider this an overdose but regardless, my mom took me to the hospital. They were very quick with me as I cried and told them I overdosed. I kept thinking of all the negative publicity addicts get on the news, and the whispers I would hear how junkies were worthless. They ran a few tests, monitored my vitals for a couple of hours, and sent me on my way.

Wouldn't you believe, when we got home she went to bed, and I did the last little bit of dope I had hid.

I was scheduled to work the following day. By 8:00 a.m. I was already going through withdrawals, even though I used the previous night at 11:00 p.m., I didn't have anything else to give my body. When I drove to work, I just kept driving and went back home. There was no way I would be able to function. I couldn't get any drugs from anyone, I didn't have any money.

I stayed in my brother's room for four days. My mom got to witness what the withdrawals were like. Heroin withdrawals were nastier and meaner than the oxy withdrawals. They both sucked, but the heroin withdrawals literally felt like I could die any minute. I couldn't eat or keep the sports drink down that my mom bought for me.

It felt like it was taking forever to get over this feeling. Four days had gone by, and I was able to get up and move around.

I decided to run to the guy's house to which I owed money for the dope and talk to him. I knew it would have only been a matter of time before he contacted me.

When I got to his house, he was shocked to see me.

"Hey, you got my money?" he asked as I shook my head no.

"Okay… well, I am sure you used all the dope, and you don't have my money. Hold on a sec."

He grabbed his roommate and stepped outside of the apartment for a minute. I had a pretty good idea of what was about to happen. I had seen him do it before. He came back in and walked towards me.

"You are going to get one," he said as I sat in the chair.

"Fine, just one, that's it," I replied as I braced myself for him to hit me.

That is what he liked to do when someone couldn't come up with his money or drugs. He would try to beat them up or get a buddy of his to help him. So that is what he did.

I sat there with my eyes closed, waiting. Then, BOOM! He hit me with a right hand, landing it directly on my left eye. He tried swinging again, but I dodged his next one and stood up.

"You better have my fucking money!"

I grabbed my keys and left. The drive home I was trying to figure out how I could come up with his money. I wasn't really concerned about getting his money because he wanted it. I wanted to get the money so I could get some more dope.

I ran home while my mom was at work and figured out a way to get some money, quickly. It involved taking some of her money. Within an hour, I had what I needed.

When I returned to his apartment, he was shocked again. I gave him his money, and then I was able to get high.

I left to go home. I was scared what my mom would do. I had stolen from her. As soon as I pulled up the rock driveway, she was waiting for me. I stepped out of the car to see my mom with a scowled look on her face, arms crossed.

"Stealing now? What the hell happened to your eye?" she asked me.

I couldn't tell her that some guy wanted his money so he hit me. I had to dress it up a bit.

"A guy I owed money to pistol whipped me," I claimed.

Her scowl suddenly turned to concern. "Wait, a gun? Why would he do that?"

My acting skills were on point that day because I really didn't want her to call the police. "He wanted his money and said I had forty-eight hours to get it to him, and then he hit me as a reminder."

I knew I had to go somewhere. I knew I had to do something different. I told her I wanted help. The look on her face and the hurt she offered me when she wanted to know about her money made me feel even like a bigger douche bag.

So that is what we did. I was able to call the place in Quincy, I was able to go to detox right away, and they rolled me over to their twenty-eight-day program.

When you are in rehab, and there is someone new coming in, it is like a new kid joining your class in grade school. You want to figure out who they are and what they like. Except in rehab, typically the first question you get asked if you are new is "What is your drug of choice?"

It was weird; the severe alcoholics sat with the alcoholics, the heroin junkies sat with the heroin junkies, etc. It is like the way we individually segregate ourselves by race or social class. We break off into groups; I guess we do that so we feel like we fit in somewhere.

Two weeks went by, and Christina, my mom, my brother, and my daughter came to visit. It was great to see them. I was feeling fabulous. I was about twenty days clean and sober and hugging them as soon as they pulled up never felt so good. When they left, I was already on the phone brokering a deal to get a bunch of Oxycontin from the guy that use to sell me the forty milligram tabs.

I was doing fantastic despite negotiating the deal. I was doing my "homework" and doing my chores. It felt good doing something productive. I couldn't understand that trying to "score" oxycontin while I was in rehab was a problem.

I had a moment with a counselor, and he asked me to name just ten good things about me. I couldn't name one. He tried telling me I was a good father. And hearing that statement reminded me of just how broken I really was – how bad of a father I was. He asked me what I wanted to do with my life. I wanted the oxycontin right then. My mom, my dad, my daughter, and my whole family felt the wrath of my destruction. I couldn't think of anything good.

I made it home. It felt good to be back, and my mom wanted me to go out to dinner with her and the family. I didn't feel like eating with everybody, so I told her I would like to stay home alone.

What was really going on is the guy I was getting the Oxycontin from was waiting at the McDonalds. When my mom left, I waited fifteen minutes until I called him to come get me.

He picked me up and we stopped by Walgreens, and in less than twenty-four hours of leaving rehab, I had a needle full of oxy going up my arm.

After a weeklong binge, everyone knew I was back on something. I was yelled at and scorned. Rightly so, I was killing myself slowly, and there was nothing my family could do about it. I started taking liquid fentanyl patches a family member had by cutting them open and drinking it. Any chance I had, I took Xanax, along with any opiates I could get my hands on to intensify the effects.

Then I did heroin again, which I swore I wouldn't. I sat in my mom's bathtub, with the door locked and a butcher's knife in hand. Tears streamed down my face so fast that I could have filled the tub. I swallowed what saliva I had in my mouth, convincing myself to end it. I couldn't go on like this any longer. I put the knife to my wrist, closed my eyes, and knock...knock. "Ty are you in there?" It was Christina's voice.

I cleared my throat, and wiped my tears away with

the bath water, "Yeah."

She jimmied the door open and came in. I hid the knife under my thigh hoping she wouldn't see it.

She had seen it, the knife that is. She stared at me for a few seconds and tried talking through her own tears. "It has gotten this bad that you want to kill yourself?"

I didn't know what to say, I didn't know what to do. It was eating me up she didn't want me, and my daughter wasn't in my life. She convinced me to give her the knife and that I needed to go to the psych ward.

I just wanted to quit feeling so horrible. I wanted to quit hating myself.

When I got to the hospital, I was nervous. I would be going through withdrawals somewhere I thought was just for "crazies" like you would see in the movies.

I remember walking down the hall to the locked door that led to the psychiatric floor. I had to remove my belt, shoelaces, and anything else that was loose.

I walked in, and there was a gentleman, sitting at a table, alone, that was hitting himself in the head over and over. Then another gentleman walked up to me. He was taller than me, probably six-feet-four, with a shaved head. His arms were lanky, and a few front teeth were missing.

"HI!" he yelled as he stood no more than a foot from my face.

I wasn't sure how to respond or what to expect. A nurse came over and escorted him to the television area. I looked at the T.V., and it was encased in Plexiglas. I wanted to leave. I thought I didn't belong there.

The nurse could see my worry and assured me I would be okay.

They showed me to my room and said I could lie down if I would like. They put me in a room with a guy who had some type of condition. He was obsessed with running water and flushing the toilet. My first night was horrible. From the withdrawals and my "roommate" flushing the toilet all night, I didn't get any sleep.

T.A. Bechel

The following day I was able to meet with the psychiatrist. He had a mustache, stood about five-feet-eight, and had a calming voice. The more we talked, the more he assured me that I could get well.

"Listen, no woman is worth killing yourself over. And if you did, your daughter wouldn't have a father, regardless how much you think you have failed. You are suffering from addiction, you are just a little mixed up, that's all," he said as he informed me that more suicides take place than there are homicides.

His demeanor reminded me of my grandma that had passed away. I felt for the first time that I could make positive changes.

After five days they released me and Christina had me move back in with her. I knew then she cared way too much for me.

Things couldn't have gotten any worse. I was doing okay. I was still drinking which was a big mistake.

I got a call from a detective regarding the money from the cell phone store. He wanted to meet. The same day Christina and I found out she was again, in fact, pregnant with our second child.

Chapter 12

Abandon Ship

I met with the detectives in an interrogation room. The mentality of just sitting in that room made me feel like a horrible violent criminal. I knew society wasn't really kind to anyone who lands up behind bars. There was a camera in the ceiling looking down on us. They were really nice, probably on the account that I was cooperating.

They were trying to coax a confession out of me regarding the money. I couldn't tell them what happened to it except that I was willing to take full responsibility. It was over within thirty minutes, the detective followed Christina and me to my mom's house where the bank bag was.

Once I handed him the bag, he advised me not to go too far and that he would be in touch.

I was nervous. I was pretty much convinced that I was going to jail forever.

Then I got the call from the detective about two weeks later. He said that I would be charged and that I would need to turn myself in that Friday.

I had never been in trouble with the law, and I was nervous I would not get to see my family. I wasn't sure what to expect.

Thursday night the detective called me and advised me to just lay low until Monday but to be sure to turn myself in on Monday.

Come Monday, I turned myself in. The detective was actually really nice and encouraged me to keep working towards getting even better. He drove me to the Madison County Jail. We drove into a dimly lit garage. It was strange; he allowed me to sit in the front seat and didn't bother handcuffing me.

He removed his gun and put it in a lock box on the wall. I couldn't believe I was going to jail. He continued to walk me through the gate after he was buzzed through. You never fully forget the sounds of the big keys jingling or the buzzer going off, unlocking the door.

I signed some of the paperwork, he whispered in my ear to just keep to myself, and it should only be about two weeks.

As he left, I felt like I lost a best friend. I was fingerprinted, and my picture was taken. Then they threw me in the holding cell until I had to do my intake.

Before I was taken back to the cell block, I had to remove all of my clothes and wash. The shower was freezing cold. I remember keeping my body protected as the officer had to watch me. I threw on my orange jumpsuit, was handed my mattress that might as well have been cardboard, my blanket, toilet paper, toothbrush, and a hotel sized bar of soap.

It was actually happening, I was going to jail. Only bad guys went to jail, I thought to myself. I didn't feel much like a criminal, but I guess in the eyes of the law I was.

They brought me to the cell block I would be staying at. They opened the main door and locked it behind us. Metal bars stood tall right in front of me - caging grown men like they were rabid animals.

The smell was gross, and my sockless feet were already cold. I arrived right before lunch, so I was lucky to get a hot meal that was a lame version of Chef Boyardee's Beef Ravioli. Some very nice fellow must have known I didn't want it so he kindly told me to give it to him.

Oh, my God. I wasn't even in jail for an hour, and I already had my food taken from me. Two weeks was going to be a long time.

The next morning my name was called. I had T.V. court. I shortly found out, since that it was my first offense, I would be let out that day.

I always over-dramatized. I kept thinking of the

movie *Carlito's Way*, starring Al Pacino when his character Carlito was finally set free. Free at last, I thought to myself.

Before dinner could be served, I was getting my belongings back and signing my paperwork to get the hell out of that hell hole.

I told myself that I would never go back.

A few court days later, I was put on probation with the opportunity to amend my felony charge to a misdemeanor under the stipulations that I complete the probation successfully.

I was trying to get back on top of the world and straighten things out with Christina. I was only drinking and taking a few pills here and there.

Then it was time. Our second child was going to come, soon. Christina's water broke when she was in the tub. We grabbed her bag and rushed her to the hospital.

The same drill happened with the machines except for this time they had to monitor the contractions right away. I was so excited to meet our second child.

A few hours went by. My hand was turned into mush again, and I didn't make any jokes this time – the demons. Then the second most beautiful sound was introduced to me that day. Our second daughter was born and cried.

She was perfect. Her eyes met mine just like her older sister's did and I knew that I had to provide a better life for the two of them.

A few months went by and things were going okay. I was taking Vic's and Xanax more than I wanted to but I was taking them from family that had them, Christina being one of them. She had a prescription of both that she rarely took.

The October following our second daughter's birth, we went to a Halloween costume party. I dressed as Jason Voorhees, I am a huge horror fan, and she dressed like a Raggedy Ann doll. When we were in the bar, I told her I was going outside to smoke. I ran to her car and opened the trunk where her pills were.

I took a handful of Vic's and Xanax. I returned, and we started fighting as usual. This would happen anytime alcohol was involved. When we returned to her house, all of the pain and suffering that I caused with our oldest daughter and Christina came out.

Flashes of the night were vague. I didn't want to make those who cared about me so upset. The only viable solution was to leave this world. She was mad at me, yelling as I ran downstairs. I grabbed a brown extension cord and secured it around the 2 x 4's. I stepped on a stool, tied the cord around my neck, and kicked the stool out from underneath me.

I dangled there, frightened. I sobered up quickly as I scratched at the cord tightly securing my neck. Christina was coming downstairs to see what I was doing and yell at me some more, and she noticed me hanging like a wind chime on a porch swaying back and forth.

I tried to plead with her to help. But all I was able to produce was a squelching noise from my throat literally being squeezed to death. The look on her face was complete terror. I heard her scream, "Mom!"

Her mom came running downstairs. She quickly ran back upstairs to get the scissors, I assume. My vision was starting to get blurry, and everyone's movements in front of me were in slow motion. Christina covered her mouth with her hands as she paced the basement floor.

Her mom was able to cut me down then I fell to the ground and gasped for air. Christina started hitting me, begging me to tell her what was wrong with me. Her mom started scolding me, reminding me that I had two daughters that loved their daddy upstairs sleeping.

Back to the psych ward I went. I somehow splintered a bone in my wrist, I guess from the fall, so the psychiatrist prescribed me Tramadol. Five days went by, and my cousin picked me up. I got an anti-depressant along with what was considered a non-narcotic pain medication at the time.

I found out that if you take five or six Tramadol together that you could get a buzz. I didn't think about heroin or any other opiates as long as I had enough Tramadol.

Thirty days or so went by, and I got a job cooking at a bar of all places. I was trying to help with the kids, and it wasn't long before I had a drink one night after work.

A week and twenty Tramadol later, I was working with a cook who bought some cocaine. I didn't think one line would hurt after work. That one line ended up being two then I started taking Vicodin again. Not even after two months of working at the bar, I was borrowing money from the waitresses to get heroin. I would go to the bathroom and do my business. I never cooked better than the times I was on heroin.

I ran out of money, quickly. Christina knew I was on the junk again and said I had to leave, again. I was back at my mom's. I was hanging out at my grandpa's a lot because I was able to borrow or work for money from him.

It wasn't long before the work dried up and I had borrowed the last dime I could squeeze out of him. My grandpa is a very, kind, hard working man that did nothing but take care of all of his children and grandchildren. But that wasn't enough for me. I knew where he kept his wallet. I would start taking twenty or forty dollars.

I was taking one hundred dollars at a time, and he knew. He moved his wallet, but I managed to always find it. Then he asked me not to come back, to leave.

I wanted to get off of the heroin, so I found someone that had a readily supply of tramadol. They would give them to me for free because they didn't realize they got you high. I was taking up to thirty a day.

When I ran out of the tramadol, I tried taking

Ibuprofen or Tylenol to ease the pain. I was taking up to a two hundred count bottle of either of the over the counter pain relievers a week. I started getting kidney stones all the time. This was an excellent way to stay on the Tramadol.

Then it became too much, and I started on heroin again. I wasn't seeing my two daughters, and I was making my mom's life a living hell. My mom had to sleep with her purse. I would take her sleeping medicine consistently along with Lyrica to dull the pain and intensify the effects. Xanax, Lyrica, Vicodin, Oxycodone, Ambien, Cymbalta, Adderall, Oxycontin, Suboxone, Methadone, and Heroin. It was kind of like the Pokemon slogan, "Gotta catch 'em all!"

I was borrowing any car I could get to drive Route 3 into the City of St. Louis. There was always a dealer to find if your regular connection wouldn't answer. You would get directed to drive somewhere and wait. They would pull up then you would follow for a few blocks.

After getting my dope, I would stop somewhere off of Salisbury and do my dose. I couldn't wait. The twenty-minute drive to St. Louis felt like an hour. I couldn't wait another twenty minutes. If I was severely paranoid that the Jump Out Boys or a random street walker would interrupt me, I would drive to the car wash right across McKinnley Bridge on the Illinois side.

I was out of money one day. I had already pawned everything I could have pawned except one item. My brother's Hoyt My Sport compound bow and arrow was up for grabs.

There were a few times I would go with people that wanted dope too and return items that they had stolen from a store, get the gift card, and sell it to a shop on Broadway in Alton. But by this time, I didn't want to share with anyone, and I didn't like taking four hours of my day to get money to get the dope I needed.

My probation was almost up, with the chance of

being revoked. I was hurting very badly, so bad that I decided to take my brother's bow and arrow with the idea to pawn it in the morning and get it back before he got off of work – ideas were always like this when you are a junkie.

I got ninety dollars for a four hundred dollar bow. I had a girl drive me to the city, and when we got back, we went to her place. When you are scoping and doping, you always want to get someone's stuff back, but it usually didn't end up that way.

This day it definitely did not. Around 2:00 p.m. I got a call from my brother three times in a row. I knew what that meant. The girl's house I was at told me to leave because I did her buttons too. As I stood in Hartford, listening to my brother on the phone, I couldn't believe what I had done.

I told him I could get his bow. Christina's mom offered to get it out for me, but he had already called the police station.

The officers needed to get the pawn ticket to get the bow and charge me with theft. I went to a detox in Southern Illinois. Six days later, I returned home to find out they were trying to charge me with Residential Burglary on my own home. I was staying at Christina's house because my brother didn't want me at my mom's, which I didn't blame him.

We hired an attorney, and he told me to lay low while he got the charge amended. I didn't listen very well. I was nervous, and the only way I could deal with the way I felt was to take something. The only thing I was able to get my hands on was Xanax. Christina asked me to leave so I found myself at my mom's.

As I sat on the swing, I was talking to Christina, explaining to her how awful I felt. I was talking crazy on the phone so my brother called the cops.

My brother told me they were coming to take me to jail. I didn't panic, maybe because I took a bunch of

Xanax or because I was at a loss. I had nowhere to go. Everyone abandoned ship.

Chapter 13

God Has Spoken

If you are still reading this, thank you. It took a lot of time to write, but the message is hidden throughout the chaos presented throughout my story. The day I heard God speak was the day a judge made it very clear of the position I was in.

I went back to jail. I first went to the city jail where I stayed for about seventy-two hours. It was worse than Madison County. Lunch one day was a can of baked beans, which was it.

I came at the same time as a guy that seemed to be a constant visitor. He was nice to talk to because he didn't judge and told me to get my life together. He also found himself inside the insane ring of drugs. He knew quite a few people I ran with at one time. He was supposed to be transported to another county so he wasn't going anywhere either.

On Sunday morning an elderly gentleman came in Bible in hand and talked to all of us. He stopped by my cell. I started crying and told him drugs have helped ruin my life. He was so forgiving with his words, he told me to shoo the devil away when he tries entering my life. We prayed that day and for the first time, I felt an ease come over me temporarily without any drugs, alcohol, or sexual distractions.

During our last twelve hours at the local jail, before they transported us to Madison County, one of the police officers thought it was funny to play Barney the Purple Dinosaur's "I Love You" song for twelve consecutive hours.

"I love you, you love me, we're a happy family. With a great big hug and a kiss from me to you. Won't you say you love me too."

"I love you, you love me, we're a happy family. With a great big hug and a kiss from me to you. Won't you say you love me too."

"I love you, you love me, we're a happy family. With a great big hug and a kiss from me to you. Won't you say you love me too."

"I love you, you love me, we're a happy family. With a great big hug and a kiss from me to you. Won't you say you love me too."

For twelve hours, this other guy and I heard this song. If you haven't been forced to listen to the same song that looped every minute, I dare you to try.

I do not know what happens to our brains, but the guy I was in there with started shaking the bars, begging them to just change the song.

My hair felt like it was going to stand up on its own on top of my head. It wouldn't stop. I cried into my pillow praying that they would stop it. He shook the bars yelling even louder.

We heard a few guys laughing, and then they turned the radio up. I felt like an unwanted, orphaned dog in a kennel that evening. I didn't feel human at all. As their laughter pierced the shred of humanity I did have left, I could only cry.

When they drove us to the jail, they let us have a cigarette. Because they felt bad? Now I am not mad at them nor was I ever. I did feel inhuman like an abused dog that hasn't eaten in days and is forced to sit in a cage and watch everyone else enjoy their meals. And please, try to not get upset and say all police officers are bad. There are many, and I mean many great cops that do make our streets amazingly safe.

I was in Madison County for two weeks before the lawyer Christina hired to prevent me from going to prison for a few years was able to get me released. He managed to get me into The Drug Court Program.

I met him at the courthouse to sign some paperwork so I could get my brother's bow out of evidence. You may be thinking that me praying with the elderly man was the voice of God, and that is what I am referring to in the name of this chapter. Nope.

When we think of God, we usually think of he, but this reference to a voice of God was a woman – a woman judge who was not afraid to tell me her thoughts. I could tell by her tone I did not want to show any signs of disrespect. She specifically enforced with her words just how hard my attorney worked to make this happen.

A few weeks later I met a man, a man that served as another voice of God who would undeniably get on my last nerve but end up becoming someone that I looked up to in the end.

I walked into the Madison County Criminal Justice Center trying to keep my composure. I pretty much failed my first probation and now, with a second chance and being to jail twice, I felt like a loser, a criminal, a convict, and a felon. And as I placed my metal objects in the bin and walked through the metal detector, that feeling only grew heavier on my mind.

I made my way up to the third floor and told the very nice woman I was there to see Mr. Blanco.

I was nervous just standing there. My last probation officer I probably met one time, never to hear from them again. My attorney told me Drug Court was relatively intense, and I would soon find out.

Mr. Blanco came and got from the waiting area, and we sat at his desk. He was really friendly and very polite. He asked me questions about drugs that I have done, my family, and if I wanted to get well. I did want to get well, very much so. He was pleased I did, but he heeded a warning that I would cross time after time.

Mr. Blanco leaned closer to me over his desk and looked straight into my eyes. "Now, Mr. Bechel, there is something you need to know. The only thing I cannot tolerate is if you lie. Don't do it. The only way we can help one another is if you are honest."

I looked directly back into his eyes. "Yes, sir." And

at the time I meant it with all of my heart.

He gave me some paperwork and told me I had to check with a mental health facility in our county and get that step done so I could be introduced to groups.

I called the facility right after I left Mr. Blanco's office and made an appointment.

When I made it to my appointment, I walked through the doors and spoke to the receptionist. All of these places I had to go (jail, a probation office, and now here) the staff all made me feel like I was just one cow in a herd that was being corralled. I allowed myself not to feel human, but I was going to change all of that.

As I sat and waited for a staff member to do my intake, a man walked through the door. He was kind of short, had a little belly, and strikingly resembled the actor Timothy Spall. If even of you have seen the movie "Rockstar" starring Mark Wahlberg, Timothy Spall plays Wahlberg's manager in the film.

We sat down in Timothy Spall's doppelganger's office and began to get to know one another. He asked me similar questions Mr. Blanco did, but he made a comment, which seriously threw me for a loop.

"I just want you to know that I am proud of you," he said as I stared, motionlessly at him.

Similar to the time that I was at rehab in Quincy, and the counselor there asked me to name ten great things about me, and what I wanted to do with my life, I was not feeling it.

"Proud of me??? WTF is he talking about. I am a G.D. loser. But I guess I will run with it. He means well I suppose." I thought to myself.

Our intake was over, I shook his hand and told him I would see him in the groups I was required to attend for Drug Court.

I started "treatment" off right. I was going to group. I was honest, and I was trying to stay off the drugs and alcohol.

Group was always weird, there was a group of men, or some may call us boys, in a room, which really didn't want to be there or share any feelings with one another.

One day we were talking about Suboxone (buprenorphine). This drug is supposed to be an opiate deterrent or with its technical term, an Opiate Replacement Therapy Drug. I use to get the little orange, hexagon shaped eight-milligram pills and crush them to get high. I usually bought them, illegally, when I was desperately trying to stay clean and sober. They helped for the time being, but I always craved the heavier drugs like heroin.

As I sat there and listened to everyone, I realized how distorted we all were. It was really bizarre. I had about sixty days clean and sober, so I was starting to understand a little bit about me and my addiction woes.

We were required to go to Twelve-Step Support Group Meetings. I went to some when I was in Quincy and didn't really like them but at Quincy, I don't think I really understood what getting clean and sober meant.

I started going to my two required meetings a week and pretty much ranted and raved about my "horrible" life. I was feeling really sorry for myself as most of us do in early recovery. I think that is not only acceptable but normal.

I didn't really like who I was, nor did I really want to share with others who I had become through the lies, stealing, and manipulating.

I made it almost ninety days clean and sober until I got kidney stones, again. If anyone has ever had kidney stones, they are not pleasant, not one bit. I went to the hospital and was able to get prescribed Vicodin. Now let me inform you that in Drug Court they pretty much do not care if your leg is falling off, you do not take any narcotics – ever.

That was the beginning of another binge. I told my counselor, Timothy Spall's doppelganger, that I had used and couldn't quit. He was able to get me into their residential facility in Bloomington during Christmas, which was hard but I knew I had to do it.

I was there twenty-eight days, I did everything I was asked, and I began understanding what it meant to get honest with the Twelve-Steps. But when you mix a bunch of "rowdy boys" together for almost twenty-four hours a day, mischief is bound to ensue.

We were not allowed to have caffeinated coffee, so at outside meetings, most of us got Mountain Dew out of the vending machine and drank as much coffee as possible. It reminded me of the dog being locked in the cage and watching everyone else eat their meals, except the dog was released and ate anything and everything he or she could sink their teeth into, not knowing when the next meal would be.

We were in and out of groups all day, keeping us busy and distracted. It wasn't a bad experience, but it wasn't enough. Twenty-eight days is not enough really for anyone who suffers from heavy addiction. Changing is just that, changing almost everything about you. But one thing I noticed is how a community, not just people in recovery, but the community we were a part of functioned.

There were many of us broken, most of us stubborn, but we all did our best to get along. The staff - some of them in recovery, some of them not - pulled together with us "residents" and made it work well.

This is where I went back to fifth grade and revisited the question my teacher asked me and visited the counselor at the Quincy facility asking me the same thing. I thought about this one day when we were in a circle as we read from a meditation book. I knew right then that everyone, even the worst cases of us, wanted to be happy.

While I was there, I got kidney stones, again. It was horrible. I did my best to suck up the pain until they passed but the staff insisted I go to the hospital. I signed paperwork stating I would not accept any narcotics which I didn't. When I left the hospital the following day, they prescribed me... tramadol! Dum...Dum...Dum... I believe tramadol is now classified as a narcotic.

My first thought was, "Well, if they prescribe it, and the treatment facility allows me to take it, maybe it isn't that bad."

That is just what I did. I was able to take four a day and one pill at a time would change my brain a little bit but enough to notice. I should have opted out, but I was in such "horrible" pain.

I completed the program and returned home to my family. Christina and I were getting along great. She didn't want me to go to Twelve-Step meetings because I was lying and taking Vicodin when I was supposed to be getting "well."

I was feeling pretty good, especially that I was able to see my children every day and lie next to Christina in bed.

This didn't last long. The craving for pills came back. I left the "honeymoon" phase of my recovery and all the demons latched back into me like an unwanted parasite. I started stealing her mom's pills and money to buy more pills.

I was again kicked out, and I had to go to my mom's.

I had to change counselors to a more constructive and stricter counselor. This counselor reminded me of a taller version of R. Lee Ermey's character, Sgt. Hartman, in Stanley Kubrick's "Full Metal Jacket." The counselor didn't have the same facial structures as Sgt. Hartman but his hair was exactly the same.

Mr. Blanco was mad that I was lying to him and Sgt. Hartman # 2 was not going to put up with my "Mickey Mouse Bullshit."

I had to take extra drug tests, and I was switched to

a different group where I spent all of my time with Hartman #2.

One day Mr. Blanco and I were having a friendly conversation, or at least I was trying. He wasn't buying it.

"Mr. Bechel, you got the gift of gab don't ya?" Mr. Blanco asked as I smoked a cigarette on our group's first break

I smiled because I thought that was a compliment. "Why yes Mr. Blanco, I do."

He had me pegged. He knew I spent many years in sales and marketing so being quick with the tongue and any rebuttal opportunity came with ease for me.

"Well, I suggest that you stop. I am going to tell you what I told you the first day we met. Stop lying and be honest with me," he said as I interrupted him.

"I will, I am just..." I attempted to say as he interrupted with getting the final word.

"Now, listen. Stop talking and listen carefully. I am seasoned, Mr. Bechel. I have been around long enough to know that you are full of crap. Get back to the group and get honest."

He hung up the phone, and I stood there in shock as I finished my cigarette. I went back to the group, under the influence of six or seven Tramadol. I did what Mr. Blanco suggested; I sat and listened.

Hartman # 2 and Mr. Blanco must have been talking about me quite frequently. After group that day I had to stay and talk with Hartman # 2.

"Grow some balls Mr. Bechel," was the last thing Hartman # 2 had said before I left for the day.

They knew I was having difficulties at home, and my mom and Christina were very reluctant of me going to any meetings.

I was mad at my probation officer, my counselor, Christina, and my mom. Nobody understood me, I thought – nobody. The best way that I dealt with this was to start using, heavily.

I started working at a restaurant as a dishwasher of all things and was miserable the whole time. I spent so much time going backward that I started hating myself all over again. I was forced to go to more Twelve Step meetings a week. I started getting Vicodin for the staff, taking some for myself. It was only a matter of time before I went back to St. Louis, this time even harder.

I started timing my drops at group. I was hiding it from mom and Christina whenever I could. Even though Christina kicked me out, she was desperately trying to help me get better.

One day, unexpectedly, Christina showed up at my mom's. She caught me sticking a needle in my arm and called Mr. Blanco.

I tried convincing her to stop calling, and she ran to her car, locked the doors, and cracked her window.

"He wants to talk to you, you liar," she said as she tried to hold back any tears.

See I put so many people through hell, literal hell.

I grabbed the phone, and I will not tell you what he said, but I will say there were a few cuss words and a "Get to court TODAY!"

Christina took me to court. I felt all of the eyes were on me. The judge had the officers put me in cuffs and shackles, and I was taken into custody for a week for my own safety.

When I was brought before the judge, she told me I had to go to a longer term treatment facility.

I ended up going to a forty-five-day facility in Mt. Vernon. Just like Bloomington and Quincy, it was pretty much the same except a counselor that reminded me of my grandpa that I had stolen from. He was one of us. He was part of a Twelve Step program.

When I had a group with him, it made sense. He spoke from experience and not a text book or something he learned from a college course. He never got mad at any of us or never made us feel insecure. He helped build us up; he was gentle yet firm with his words.

He had taught us how to do the Two-Step dance. He played dancing music on the radio. One song really hit home for me. The Glenn Miller Band's song "Honors Us Troops" played from this counselor's CD player. My grandpa, who I had stolen from, used to play this song and try to teach my cousins and me the Two-Step when we were younger.

Suddenly memories of my grandpa, his black goatee and all, came back of him dancing on his hardwood floor, and his arms moving back and forth, with a smile on his face as my cousins and I watched his joy. His joy was our joy, and I think that goes for most children.

I did very well here too. I did the chores that I was assigned to do. But this time with Christina, things were getting weird. When we would talk on the phone, she was short with her words - always quick to pass the phone to my mom.

I knew this tone, this behavior – she was talking to another guy.

I finally asked her about it one day during a phone conversation. I was torn when I heard her words. She wasn't dating him. She was just talking to him. I wasn't mad at her; I was mad at myself. I didn't blame her one bit. She stuck by my side when she should have run the other way. She should have deleted me from her memory bank, never to think of me again.

I completed the program without any problems. Christina was the one that picked me up and the hour long ride, I couldn't help but think that things were going to get worse for us. I was going to lose her completely – forever.

I came back to group, the judge was happy, and I started getting honest until one day I thought I could do heroin one last time. I thought to myself, "I am doing great. I can get one last hoorah and no one would have to know."

I went on a bender once again. I disappeared from group for a whole week. Christina would not return any of my calls. I took my mother hostage in her own home – not literally. I came and went as I pleased. I stole fifty dollars from her, and she didn't want to call the police and send me to jail. She should have. Then after my week bender, I had a guy who went in on some dope with me stay the night at my mom's house. He was in the same position I was. His family was at a loss, and they didn't know what to do except for banishing him until he got better.

My mom was getting ready for work and yelled from her room, "He better be outta here by the time I leave, or I am calling the cops."

The guy shot up from the couch, quickly put on his shoes, and left.

As I laid flat on the couch in the living room, I stared at the ceiling fan. I thought of the ceiling fan in my grandma's room the day she passed away. I thought of my children. I thought of anything I could latch onto that would take me away from ending my life.

My mom was leaving for work, and she had only one thing to say. "I do not want to see you here tonight. So be gone when I get off."

As soon as she left, I sat up from the couch. I started crying tears of nothing but hopelessness and desperation.

I fell to my knees, barely able to breathe as I gasped for air looking for an answer. "Please," I pleaded through my clenched teeth, "help me." I couldn't quit crying.

I started taking both fists and hitting my forehead over and over. "I can't do this on my own. If I have something, anything to offer this world, then help me," I screamed at the top of my lungs, "help me."

I fell to the floor and moved to a fetal position. As I laid there, I wanted to die. Voices were no longer whispers they were screaming, telling me to end it.

Then my phone rang. I knew the number. It was Mr.

Blanco. "Why are you not at group again?"

I was silent; I had no words to offer him.

"Because you didn't want to go that's why," he said.

I sat there and knew he was right. I didn't want to go. I didn't want to live either. I told him I was going to go to detox.

"Detox, that's fine, but when you get back, you are going to turn yourself in."

That is what I did. I convinced my mom to drive me to Mt. Vernon for a five-day detox. I returned home and spent the night with Christina and my two daughters then the following day I went to the Madison County Jail and pressed the buzzer to get an officer's attention.

I wasn't stressed about being in jail, I was actually relieved. I met a lot of great people in jail - a lot of angry and misunderstood people of all races. I observed everyone there over the course of two weeks I was there. They all wanted to be part of something, a group. They all wanted to laugh and enjoy something like me. At this moment, as I watched the guys fill a picnic table bolted down to the floor play Spades, I realized how much alike all of us are on the planet. I didn't have to fight any longer.

I was called before the judge. She thanked me for turning myself in as she followed with my final three options. Option 1: Be put on termination, go to support meetings every day and see how I was in thirty days. Option 2: Go to a three to six-month recovery house in our county. Option 3: Go to a six-month to two-year recovery home in a neighboring county.

I didn't hesitate. My mind was made up in less than five seconds. I knew of the recovery home in the neighboring county and I chose to go there.

I was released from jail and spent a week with my family before a really nice fellow that loves the sport rugby drove me up to the recovery home.

When I arrived, I was very accepting of the

conditions. The recovery house was an old school, which was falling apart, but had so much to offer inside those broken and cracked walls. Many of the residents thought I was crazy because I was always happy and willing to help out around what we called our house.

At this home, they had a food pantry for the public where we distributed food every Friday. We were able to volunteer at an animal shelter to help other creatures that were alone and broken. The house also housed one dog at a time as we were considered a foster home for the dog until he or she could get adopted. We had to do flag honor and put up the flag and take it down, folding it military style. We had to cook for one another – someone always complained about the food.

I started putting together the grocery list every week and going to the store with a guy who worked in the office who I became great friends with.

We had support meetings almost every day. I met my first mentor I was honest with. J.G. was a life saver, never judging me of my past. He was gentle but firm with his words like the counselor from Mt. Vernon.

Christina visited me literally every weekend. We laughed, we cried, and sometimes got mad at one another. She would bring our daughters too. There was a gymnasium in the building. Though the paint was peeling and the concrete floor was cracking, my kids and I played basketball, tag, and tennis. We would take walks and go to the park when they visited.

I started going outside at night and talking to the stars and listening the best I could. I read, I wrote in my journal, I ate and tasted my food. I made my bed every single day. I washed my own clothes and folded them. I showered every day and brushed my teeth.

I would sit up late at night with my "pod mates" and make dirty jokes, but laugh like I hadn't laughed in a very long time. I gave hi-fives, fist bumps, and offered encouraging words for anyone who was a new resident.

While I was there, I was reminded of how serious this addiction business is. One person left because she was still drinking. She ran off with a male resident because they liked each other. She was dead within two months of leaving.

I didn't want to die any longer. I wanted to live, laugh, learn, and most importantly, love. My purpose was forming right then and there. Purpose takes time for most of us. The thing is my purpose, and it isn't done forming, but as each day passes and I stay clean and sober, my purpose gets stronger and more positive. Authenticity and discernment are values I treasure today.

I have not touched drugs or alcohol since I broke down in tears and crawled into the fetal position that day.

I realize that we, humans that is, are only on the verge of life as we know it. I was broken. Sometimes the only way we start making sense of all of this is when we begin to examine the broken pieces and gradually put them back together again.

Chapter 14

Our Work is Never Done

As I put together the past and recounted everything I put everyone through, some parts were difficult to write. I brought back to life the past that I have forgiven myself for, but revisiting the streets of St. Louis became real all over again. I could see the streets, the sun glaring off the hood of the car I was traveling in, the smell of the spoon, and the pain that flowed through me.

We are facing something bigger than a heroin epidemic. I will not bore you with statistics, but I will remind anyone reading this that many prominent medical officials are claiming drug and alcohol addiction to be the BIGGEST threat to humanity in the twenty-first century. That is a bold claim, but a claim that doesn't run from reality like I did.

Today I am the happiest I have ever been. Please don't think I am perfect, for that I am not. I still get angry, I still must apologize, and I must start my morning every day with the direction of positive thoughts.

I am a firm believer we are all time travelers. We are supposed to remember the past, not to be controlled by it, but to learn from it and help others from our experience. I believe the future is of our own making as we must spend just enough time there before we move from dreamers to fantasizers. We find our balance, our reality, in today. Some of us fantasize about our future to try to reconcile our past.

I have a tattoo on my forearm. It says, "Mitakuye Oyasin." As www.wolfwalkercollection.com provides, it is translated as this:

"Aho Mitakuye Oyasin... All my relations. I honor you in this circle of life with me today. I am grateful for this opportunity to acknowledge you in this prayer...

To the Creator, for the ultimate gift of life, I thank you.

To the mineral nation, which has built and maintained my bones and all foundations of life experience, I thank you.

To the plant nation, which sustains my organs and body, and gives me healing herbs for sickness, I thank you.

To the animal nation, which feeds me from your own flesh and offers your loyal companionship in this walk of life, I thank you.

To the human nation, who shares my path as a soul upon the sacred wheel of Earthly life, I thank you.

To the Spirit nation, which guides me invisibly through the ups and downs of life and for carrying the torch of light through the Ages, I thank you.

To the Four Winds of Change and Growth, I thank you.

You are all my relations, my relatives, without whom I would not live. We are in the circle of life together, co-existing, co-dependent, co-creating our destiny. One, not more important than the other. One nation evolving from the other and yet each dependent upon the one above and the one below. All of us a part of the Great Mystery.

Thank you for this Life."

I have never been a fan of the term "strive for perfection." Perfection is not real. We may be able to get close but never obtain it – it is a farce. Today I strive for love. Love is what connects us. Love is what binds us. Most importantly, love is what can heal us.

Hate disconnects us. Hate is what divides us. Hate most importantly is what will defeat us.

I do not strive to be the best, I strive to be better. I have so many improvements to make in exercising, meditating, being a father, a companion, a son, and a friend. And striving and working towards love is what is getting me there. If I keep doing what I am doing, I will have four years clean and sober in a few months after finishing this. It has been three years since I have smoked a cigarette and taken any anti-depressants. I live healthier than I ever have, from the food I eat to the exercise that I do. Cardio helps me more with depression than any narcotics or anti-depressants could. Doctors at one time tried desperately to convince me to take an Opiate Replacement Drug like Suboxone, Methadone, or Vivitrol. I didn't want to replace one drug for another – seemed ridiculous to me. I listen to great bands to remind me to continue working on becoming even better like Nahko and Medicine for the People, Xavier Rudd, etc., but I am still a fanatic of metal music.

I want to write. I have wanted to be a writer of fiction since I won a Young Author's Award in the second grade. I practice every day through reading and writing. I told the director at the recovery home that I would write. And write I have. Not only have I written titles like "Origins of a Boy Named Luci" and "Bullied to the Death," but I have also created some poems that are a little more sensitive than my horror-fiction. I would have never guessed that I would be courageous enough to share my life with the public I so desperately wanted to end using drugs on more than one occasion. Anyone that has read this far, I thank you. "Change is constant, why not make it positive." – T.A. Bechel

About The Author

T.A. Bechel, an Illinois native, is a writer of fiction, consisting of horror and thriller titles like Bullied to the Death, Origins of a Boy Named Luci, A Happy Death, The White Haystack, and Cercueil. Father of four children, two girls and two boys, T.A. Bechel, decided to bring his struggle with drugs and alcohol to life by offering transparency in the most intimate fashion by penning his highly anticipated autobiography, Heroin Rising: A Tale of True Terror.

Samples of My Work

Two Birds

Two birds perched on a wire,
One chirps to the other, "What is it you desire?"
"I want a nest constructed of gold."
"I want to know every secret ever told."
"I want all of the world's power."
"I want to look down on my subject from the highest tower."
"I want to be the most handsome bird in all the land."
"I want a beautiful island with palm trees and white sand."
"I want all the food I can eat."
"I want to be the one to lead the fleet."
"Oh, enough about me as we are perched on this wire,"
The other bird chirps, "What is it you desire?"
"I desire none of those silly things."
"I want to fly and soar, why else would I be given wings."

Origins of a Boy Named Luci

(Excerpt)

Present Day

Luci has never experienced fear, but that is what he is feeling now. Sweat beading on his red tinted forehead as he gasps for oxygen, Luci fears that he can no longer help his friends or family. Struggling to breathe, he keeps running. Each footstep hits the ground harder and faster as each breath swells his lungs. He looks over his shoulder to see if he has created enough distance between him and the mob chasing after him. He ran so fast for so long that the crowd has either retreated, or he has successfully evaded them.

Luci stops running. He places one hand on a tree that is firmly rooted in the earth beneath his feet. He can feel the tree's life assisting in calming him and attempting to heal him. He begins to calm, but he is not healing. One of the angry protesters pierced his back with a knife, and the blood has become thick with clots as his wound is still open. The stinging sensation is unbearable as Luci can think of only one other solution. He begins to use his power to attempt to cauterize the wound. He closes his eyes, takes a deep breath through his nostrils, and rubs his hands together as they begin to glow amber orange. He has never warmed his hands to a temperature that can burn but to close this massive cut and stop the bleeding, he must. He takes one hand and places it on his side as he takes the other and throws it around his torso to cover his wound. He presses as hard as he can to burn the opening. Tears escaping his eyes, the pain of closing the wound only adds to his misery. His people have abandoned him; he has been banished. As he screams, the smell of burnt flesh fills the air. Smoke begins to escape through his fingers as they twitch wanting to recoil from the pain.

"Ahhhhhh," he screams, "what is going on?"

He has stopped the bleeding as he begins to weep uncontrollably.

"My people, why have they forsaken me? What has Jessie done to them that is so convincing that they would not hear reason from my tongue?" he yells.

With both hands in aggravation, he grabs his hair but suddenly pulls them back into his sight. In disbelief, he looks at his palms as clumps of hair have stuck to them.

"What is happening?"

Falling to the ground, he sits with his knees bent as each arm rests on them and his hands dangle over the knee caps. As he looks around at the forest, a new and strange thought enters his mind. His thought is to die. Death in his world comes naturally – when it is time to go. Death never comes to someone by their own hands.

A mysterious voice tries soothing Luci.

"No worries child."

"Who are you?" Luci screams.

"Hate is something Jessie is after. It's his ultimate goal."

"Where are you?" Luci asks.

He looks around to see where the voice is coming from.

"I am with you. I am you," the voice says.

Confused, he continues to investigate with curiosity as a look of nervousness covers his whole face.

"What? You are me? That makes no sense. Who are you?" Luci demands.

"I am what you would call the voice of the universe. I am a sanctuary when you or someone needs comforting. That is what I am rather than whom," the voice politely answers.

A popping noise comes from the trees in front of Luci as green sparks begin falling to the ground. He watches carefully as the sparks get bigger, and the noise gets louder.

"What the..."

The smoke clears as the wind gains strength, carrying it off to be forgotten. Standing before Luci is an owl. Taking its brown and black wings, the owl dusts off its chest that is full of dried grass and dirt.

"Where did you come from?"

Luci, still sitting on the ground, kicks his feet, moves his hands, crawling backward to get away from the bird.

"All around you," the owl replies.

Hopping towards him, Luci freezes. "Get away from me."

With his back pinned against a tree and nowhere to go, the owl hops on Luci's stomach. They look into each other's eyes. Luci calms instantly as they speak to one another without spoken words. The owl breaks the silence to answer the questions that could be heard in Luci's thoughts.

"Jessie is no man. He is a black entity that craves the destruction of our world. He comes from a dark universe that consumes bright, warm, and loving balls of energy like you."

The owl jumps up and down on Luci's stomach and continues to speak. Luci's mouth is wide open, he continues to listen.

"Our universes are all dark but full of bright stars trying to guide the way. Jessie, as he calls himself, sees our planet as a threat to his kind. He cannot destroy us swiftly for he grows stronger and fiercer as the darkness grows on Earth and in all of the inhabitants. He cannot fully penetrate you because you are equally powerful but a polar opposite. He will not directly attack you but will destroy you from within without lifting one finger in aggression. He will allow hate to enter the hearts of our brothers and sisters as he has already begun to do so."

Luci looks at the owl as he uses his hands to adjust his position on the ground. His hand gets wet from a small puddle as he looks down. The ripples calm and Luci stares at his reflection. His skin is red on his right side, one horn is piercing through his forehead, and his hair is starting to fall out. As Luci reflects, he can think of only one question for this owl.

"What do I do to send him back to his universe?"

The owl flaps his wings in excitement.

"You keep preaching love to earn the trust of your people – you are the light. They will follow you once again, and you will extinguish his evil force," the owl proclaims.

Luci blinks and smiles at the owl. He takes his two hands and starts to pet the soft feathers. He looks into the owl's eyes.

"You know you are right. Jessie is somehow disfiguring me," he says as he keeps running his hands over the owl.

Luci cocks his head as his smile disappears. Grabbing the wings of the owl, he pulls with equal force as he rips them from the body. Blood shoots from each open wound where wings once were. The owl's eyes widen.

"Luci, what is wrong?" he asks as Luci shows no remorse.

Taking one hand, Luci wraps it around the owl's bony neck and squeezes so tightly that the owl's eyes begin to bulge. Blood runs off of the beak and the eyeballs dangle from their now empty sockets.

"Forget the light. Jessie wants darkness; I'll give him an eternal life of burning and suffering." Luci declares as he stands up, tossing the owl's carcass aside.

He looks back at his reflection in the puddle as he adjusts his black bow-tie that accompanies his tuxedo.

"Jessie wants a war, well he's got one. I'm coming for you." Luci yells as he walks towards town leaving a trail of fire with each footstep.

A Happy Death

I just returned home from a trip to South America. I believed I found what I thought would be the answer to my insouciance.

I walked through my front door excited to put, what I considered Pandora's Box, to the test. My clock on the wall shouted ten chimes. As much as I hated that clock's redundancies, there it clung. That's my life – I complain about everything but do nothing to change, until now.

I threw my bags and rushed to sit in my recliner. I was wheezing from being sixty pounds overweight and needing my inhaler. Being a fat guy with asthma is another cause of my self-inflicted misery.

I reached into my pocket and felt the coarse hair tickle my palm – wrapped my hand around it and could feel the energy. I would finally be able to end my self-created despondency. The whole flight home I kept thinking what I could wish for – money, girlfriend, respect, happiness. My heart raced as I fully withdrew the monkey's paw from my pocket.

I stared with reverence. The possibilities could be life changing as rapacious thoughts infected my mind. I couldn't wait any longer - I made my first wish.

"I wish for a beautiful woman to love me," I yelled.

The paw got so hot I dropped it. As it hit the floor, the index finger fell off, crumbling to dust.

I looked around – no woman. Five minutes went by – my excitement was morphing into disappointment.

Suddenly my phone alerted me that I had a text. My phone read the contact name Babe and the message said, "I'll be home in a few. Love you."

As I pondered the unsuspecting text, I heard keys fondling the front door lock. The door creaked opened. "Riker, honey. I'm home."

I was in a state of shock. I wasn't sure exactly what to say or even do. During the moment of brain glitches, she walked around the corner. Her legs ran for miles before meeting her perfectly designed hips. Her olive tone was pure perfection with no visible blemishes. Her black hair was short, tailing under her ear, displaying a bob style cut. She had green eyes that seduced you with her stare.

"Honey, hey it's Jastine. Earth to Riker," she said as she drew closer.

In a trance, mouth agape, I admired her beauty. I never knew how to speak to women, so I muttered, "Come give daddy some sugar."

She approached and straddled me as she began kissing the nape of my neck. Within seconds of her moist mouth making first contact a celebration was happening within my hormones.

She whispered in my ear, "Touch me, I want you."

My hand graciously found her pubic region and it was hot with negating extremities. I grabbed something hard and throbbing.

I looked at her, him, holy shit it was a guy.

"Get off of me," I screamed.

"Riker you said me being transgender wouldn't bother you. I promise you're going to pay," she said as a tear slipped down her cheek.

It became stronger, pinning both of my arms down against the armrest of the recliner. Its face looked like melting wax -crimson flesh fell into my lap.

I somehow freed my right arm.

"I want you, make love to me," it said as the fingernails turned into fungus infested claws.

I reached for the paw; I fumbled it but secured it. Instantly I made a wish. "I wish no beautiful woman loved me!"

Again the paw became hot, it fell as the middle finger detached, turning to dust.

She didn't disappear. Jastine screamed louder, "If you're not going to love me then it's time to DIE!"

I noticed the closet door open in front of us. Wheezing, I managed to push her in. Slamming it closed, I took a nearby chair shoving it under the handle.

The guardian of the paw said there would be unexpected consequences. I gave him ten thousand dollars, never thinking of any.

I ran to the kitchen to get my inhaler and made another wish.

"I wish for everyone to like me."

I let the paw fall before burning my palm - it hit the floor as the ring finger crumbled turning to dust.

Within a minute I heard thud....thud... all around my house. I heard from the closet and outside, in unison, "Brains, brains, ahh...ughhh."

I ran to the window, there had to be a hundred zombies. I ran to the bedroom window, another hundred zombies. I ran to the closet. Jastine bellowed, "Brains.Brains."

The sound of breaking glass and weakening wood drove chills down my back. I was in panic – I ran to the kitchen as fast as I could. I scooped the paw off the floor, making my way to the front door.

"I just wish to be HAPPY!"

I fell to the floor paralyzed. The lecherous sounds for brains were replaced with faint noises. All I could hear were men screaming, gun shots and a monkey in distress.

"Get that bastard."

"He's swinging everywhere."

"Ooohh...eeehh," the monkey cried.

"Give me that gun," a man said as gunshots were fired.

I could hear their footsteps snapping twigs with each step.

"Thanks, you slimy chimp," he said.

The door creaked open.

I heard footsteps that resembled a barefooted baby stepping on linoleum slowly approaching me.

I could only look forward - something stepped on

my chest, entering my line of sight.

A monkey! He whispered, "Remember when you said you'll be happy when you're dead. Humans are all the same. Farewell."

He picked up his paw and attached it to his wrist. He said one last thing, "He's all yours boys and girls."

The zombies gathered around me like a pride of lions. My flesh being peeled sounded like a Velcro wallet being opened.

I complained until the end. The last thing I heard was twelve chimes - indicating the stroke of midnight. Talk about an untimely death - Fucking clock.